The Capitol P
to offer the reprint of
Guide Book that desc
mosaics located throu

MW00831020

corridors. For the first time, visitors to the Capitol will be able to use a map that shows the location of the mosaics as they tour the floor that depicts Pennsylvania's history in clay tile.

With the exception of a new cover and introduction, this guidebook has been reprinted exactly as Mercer himself released it in 1908. As you walk the floor, some discrepancies between the guidebook and the floor may become evident. The Committee has left the discrepancies in the booklet unchanged in order to maintain the integrity of Mercer's original work.

The Capitol Preservation Committee would like to thank the many people who helped with the production of this publication, including, but not limited to: the Publication Subcommittee members and staff; Vance Koehler at the Bucks County Department of Parks and Recreation and Corey Amsler at the Mercer Museum for assistance with the history of the tile; Lisa Soderberg and Alex Rice at Vitetta Group, for work on the floor survey and CAD drawings; and Brian Hunt, photographer.

We invite you to take the time to visit our beautiful Capitol and enjoy the art and craftsmanship of the Moravian Tile floor with each step you take.

Paul I. Clymer, Chairman

Ruthann Hubbert-Kemper, Director

INTRODUCTION

In September 1898, Henry C. Mercer (1856-1930) founded the Moravian Pottery and Tile Works in his Bucks County hometown of Doylestown, Pennsylvania. Tile making came to Mercer as a result of his efforts to preserve aspects of American material culture that were quickly disappearing due to the continuing effects of the Industrial Revolution. Replacement of hand tools with machines and handicrafts with assembly lines was dooming the remnants of colonial arts and crafts that played an important role in forming this nation. Mercer recognized the historical and educational potential of those tools and trades being discarded and sought to preserve them.

Educated at Harvard and the University of Pennsylvania, Mercer had entered the legal profession following family tradition. Dissatisfied with the law and with his appetite for antiquities stimulated by travels abroad, he immersed himself in history, anthropology, and archaeology. In 1894, he was appointed curator of American and Prehistoric Archaeology at the University of Pennsylvania Museum and participated in several archaeological digs. The frustrations encountered in studying the distant prehistoric record strengthened an active interest in collecting artifacts of the more recent past. "Archaeology...turned me into a potter," Mercer later recalled.

During his lifetime, Mercer amassed nearly 25,000 items representative of life in early America that are now housed in the Mercer Museum of the Bucks County Historical Society. Saddened by the prospect that "so beautiful an art as that of the old Pennsylvania German potter should perish before our eyes," in the fall of 1897, Mercer briefly apprenticed himself to a Bucks

County redware potter in hopes of learning the local craft traditions. Although disappointed with his early attempts at making dishes and bowls, Mercer was ignited with enthusiasm and set out to "master the potter's art and establish a pottery under personal control." With personal financial resources and headstrong determination, he succeeded in establishing a tile factory the following year.

Mercer referred to his new venture as an "artistic pottery" and patterned his early tiles on models gathered from a large number of historic sources, such as Pennsylvania German stove plates, English, French and German medieval tiles, and objects collected during his travels in Europe and North Africa. Besides the desire to utilize local clay, Mercer's strongest assertion about tile making was a belief that tiles should be made by hand and not by machinery. He developed his own methods of producing tiles "cheap enough to sell and artistic enough to rival the old ones." His tiles retained the look and individuality of the hand process, although effectively made in quantities large enough to make them affordable. Plaster molds were used because they allowed a sufficient amount of hand work, but also allowed the integrity of Mercer's original shapes and designs to be perpetuated from worker to worker with minimal losses.

Mercer met with immediate success and his tiles were sought by leading architects who installed them in public and private buildings across the country. He became a leading figure of the American Arts and Crafts movement and his influence was far-reaching, affecting so many other tile makers well into the twentieth century. Although he did not train a group of disciples or write extensively about his tile making philosophy, Mercer did reach a following through the visibility of his products.

In August of 1903, Mercer received the most significant commission of his entire tile career, one that set off a heightened period of artistic creativity and clarified his purposes as a tile maker. The commission to provide 16,000 square feet of pavement tiles for the great rotunda and corridors for the new State Capitol Building in Harrisburg was the largest his small company ever received. The architect, Joseph Huston of Philadelphia, originally had envisioned a pictorial floor of polished colored marble, laid out in an arrangement of banded, geometrical shapes. Mercer, however, met with Huston and proposed that rough textured red tiles would contrast with the white marble walls to the advantage of each. Earlier that same year, Mercer had patented a process for making flat tile pictures, or mosaics. He claimed "[the] only analogy to the work known…being found in the earlier stained-glass windows where the pieces of glass, cut out in somewhat the same way as these pieces of clay, are welded together with bands of lead, just as these units are welded together with rather broad joints or bands of cement."

After being awarded the commission, Mercer seized this opportunity to express himself in a unique way. He set about designing subjects for approximately 400 mosaics to be interspersed amid a vast field of red three-inch quarries. For the first time, he departed from his reliance upon historical precedents and developed designs wholly based on his own experiences and creativity. He chose as his general theme the history of Pennsylvania, and realized that his tiles could tell stories, a realization that would affect so much of his later efforts.

In the preliminary notes for his guidebook, Mercer wrote: "If they [the mosaics] are not decorative they are a failure artistically. If they are only decorative, they go no further than would mere pleasing patches of color. But, if, as has been contended, they reasonably express, within the limits of the craft which produced them, facts and events in the history of Pennsylvania and the life of its inhabitant...then the pavement may claim a not unworthy part in the full significance of the building."

Although the arrangement seems random, the mosaics are, in fact, very thoughtfully placed in the floor. The tile sequence is roughly chronological. Beginning at one end of the floor with scenes depicting the Native Americans, the mosaics progress into the story of European habitation in the New World and eventually encompass the Commonwealth's triumph through process and invention. "It is the life of the people," Mercer wrote, "rough, powerful, and absolutely real, that seems to struggle in this plastic pavement for expression."

In 1908, Mercer wrote and published at his own expense his *Guide Book to the Tiled Pavement in the Capitol of Pennsylvania* so that visitors to the new building could read along as they strolled through the corridors and the great rotunda. Each mosaic had a significant story to tell and Mercer thought these stories and his artistic intentions had to be communicated. Unavailable for many years, this reprinted guidebook is a useful tool in understanding the history of Pennsylvania, as well as a record of this very important Arts and Crafts masterpiece.

Vance Koehler
Curator of Historic Property
Bucks County Department of
Parks and Recreation

When facing the Grand Staircase in the Capitol rotunda, it is common to reference "north" and "south" as points of direction. However, to avoid confusion between Mercer's Guide Book and map, the original "left" and "right" orientations have been used.

Please note: the following mosaics are listed in Mercer's original guidebook, but are not visible today.

LOCATION	NUMBER	NAME
Left Outer Corridor	#272	Ceremonial Stone
Left Lobby	#237	Crow
Left Lobby	#331	Potter Terrapin
Rotunda	#73	Stove Plate
Rotunda	#74	Kingfisher
Rotunda	#84	Gridiron
Rotunda	#85	Quail
Rotunda	#130	Wild Duck
Rotunda	#139	Keystone
Cross Lobby	#373	Battleship
Right Corridor	#330	Spider
Right Corridor	#331	Indian Brooch
Right Corridor	#403	Rabbit
Right Corridor	#404	Rattlesnake
Right Corridor	#405	Mole
Right Corridor	#406	Crab
Right Corridor	#407	Box Tortoise
Right Corridor	#408	Weasel
Right Corridor	#409	Indian Carving
Right Corridor	#410	Indian Carvings
Right Corridor	#411	Rock Carving
Right Corridor	#412	Raccoon
Right Corridor	#413	Indian Turtle
Right Corridor	#414	Eel
Right Corridor	#415	Bullfrog
Right Corridor	#416	Indian Panther
Right Corridor	#417	Grasshopper
Right Corridor	#418	Song Sparrow
Right Corridor	#419	Indian Carving
Right Corridor	#420	Kingfisher

In addition, mosaics 298, 283, 295, 291, 282, 296, 284, 297, and 292 are shown on the map, but are now covered by carpeting.

Capitol Preservation Committee Members

Chairman
Representative Paul I. Clymer

Vice Chairman
John R. Bowie
Governor's Appointee

Secretary
Eugene L. DiOrio
Governor's Appointee

Treasurer
Speaker Matthew J. Ryan
Pennsylvania House of
Representatives

Fred Belardi
Pennsylvania House of
Representatives

P. Michael Sturla
Pennsylvania House of
Representatives

Gibson E. Armstrong
Pennsylvania Senate

Leonard J. Bodack
Pennsylvania Senate

Harold F. Mowery, Jr.
Pennsylvania Senate

John N. Wozniak
Pennsylvania Senate

Beatrice Garvan
Governor's Appointee

Brent D. Glass
Executive Director, Historical
and Museum Commission

John Gedid
Supreme Court Appointee

Kelly Powell Logan
Secretary, Department of
General Services

Administrative Staff

Executive Director
Ruthann Hubbert-Kemper

Controller/Personnel
Supervisor
Sue A. Ellison

Preservation Project Managers
David L. Craig
Christopher R. Ellis
Barbara H. Strobridge

Research Historian
Jason L. Wilson

Communications Specialist
Richard E. Saiers

Computer Systems
Administrator
Daniel E. Markle

Administrative Support
John Blessing
Tara A. Pyle
Carla E. Wright

Publications, Prints and Posters of much of the artwork in the
Capitol are available for purchase. A list and order form may be
obtained by contacting:

Capitol Preservation Committee
Main Capitol Building
Harrisburg, PA 17120-0028
(717) 783-6484 / Fax (717) 772-0742
http://cpc.leg.state.pa.us

Guide Book

TO THE

Tiled Pavement

IN THE

Capitol of Pennsylvania

Guide Book

TO

The Tiled Pavement

IN THE

Capitol of Pennsylvania

BY

Henry C. Mercer.

Each mosaic in the pavement is numbered with a number stamped upon one of the square red background tiles close to the *bottom sides* or *top* of the mosaic. And each picture in this Guide Book is numbered to correspond with the number of the mosaic it illustrates. *The numbers are not set in numerical sequence.*

To find the description of a given mosaic in the Guide Book first observe its stamped number on the pavement then turn to the page indicated for this number in the numerical reference list of the mosaics on pages 1 and 2.

A number of the mosaics have been repeatedly duplicated. A few have been numbered by mistake with numbers duplicated on other mosaics, or by numbers stamped within the limits of the mosaics themselves. These can be identified by their illustrations. Several mosaics whose numbers may or may not appear have been concealed under candelabra and other objects.

Notice.

The sequence of the pictures in the Guide Book follows the chronological sequence of the mosaics on the pavement.

In order to follow the mosaics in chronological sequence, approach the Capitol in front, and enter it, not at the main middle doorway, but at the left wing entrance. Follow the mosaics across the areas of pavement by way of this entrance proceeding inwards and from left to right.

The words *right* and *left* applied to areas of pavement in this Guide Book refer in direction to corridors, lobbies and vestibules situated to the right or left hand of an individual entering the Capitol by the main (middle) front entrance.

Price 25 Cents.

Preface.

The pavement, intended to contrast in its rough texture and dominant red color with the smooth white marble walls of the Capitol, consists of upwards of four hundred plaques or mosaics, made of colored burned clay, set irregularly without borderings, against a background of small hand-made and widely-jointed red tiles. The patterns are made of large clay units, the outlines of which often help to delineate the design, as in the case of stained glass windows where pieces of glass, of varying size and shape, are set together with bands of lead, just as these units are set together with rather broad joints of cement.

Varying considerably in size, but generally not more than five feet in diameter, or gauged so as to focus the human eye at a distance of five or six feet, the mosaics may stand for mere patches of harmonious color to the individual who rapidly walks across them, while it is only to him who pauses and studies them carefully that their full significance gradually appears. What the observer sees is less a picture than a decoration. The drawing is simplified so as to satisfy the clay process. The colors of men, animals and objects are fantastic and not realistic. The skies may be red, the water black, the trees yellow.

Yet, though the result may please the eye and adorn the floor, the mosaics are intended to be not only thus decorative, but significant, reasonably expressing, within the limits of the craft which produced them, facts and events in the history of Pennsylvania and the life of its inhabitants.

Beginning at the north (left) vestibule with the Indian making fire, chipping arrow heads, paddling his boat, smoking tobacco, cultivating Indian corn, with typical inscriptions from his rock carvings and examples of his implements in stone, we pass to the European colonists felling the forest and building the log cabin, spinning, weaving, and cooking in the open fire, and to thoughts of the mining of coal, iron and petroleum. Thence, by way of great resultant developments in the form of blast furnaces, oil wells, locomotive engines, manufactures, and the manipulation of iron, we reach the symbols of today in the telegraph, trolley and automobile. To preserve continually the memory of the forest from which the State takes its name, the leaves of trees and the forms of reptiles, birds and animals frequently appear. Historical events are not omitted, but take a minor place.

It is the life of the people that is sought to be expressed; the building of a commonwealth economically great, by the individual work of thousands of hands, rather than by wars and legislatures; the successful toil, the energy and self reliance of a number of Europeans, who, taking possession of a rich and fertile region, dispossessed a weaker race, removed an all-pervading forest, contended with the forces of nature, constructed a government, and dug up and utilized the riches of the soil.

Numerical Reference List.

Numbers here set in numerical sequence to the left of the mosaic names, correspond with mosaic numbers stamped in the pavement. Numbers to the right of the mosaic names, refer to the pages in this Guide Book containing illustrated descriptions of the mosaics pertaining to their stamped numbers.

Numerical Reference List.

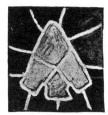

248

Arrowhead. 248. The Indian quarried jasper in the Lehigh hills at Vera Cruz, Macungie and Wieder's Run. At Macungie he excavated pits, sometimes 19 feet deep, digging over and disturbing several acres of the earth to this depth with stone spades and pointed poles, often cracking the native rock with fires built upon it, to obtain the raw material for the point of his all-important arrow.

Indian Grooved Stone Axe. 268.
The cutting edge of the pebble or other hard stone, formed into the required axe shape by pecking with another stone and rubbing smooth, is necessarily dull. Hence to cut down a tree with one of these axes mounted upon a twisted withe, the Indian first charred the lower trunk with fires built around the base of the tree.

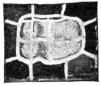

268

257

Ceremonial Mask Amulet. 257. One of the masks, grotesque, frightful, diabolic, worn in ceremonies by priests of the Lenni Lenape or Delaware Indians, is here represented from an original of wood two or three inches long, with human face carefully carved and polished, furnished with Venetian glass-bead eyes, and consequently made after contact with white men. Still preserved in Philadelphia, the amulet was presented to the family of its present owner by Tedyuscung, the Delaware chief.

Oak Leaves. 86. Long lived, colossal, durable, with color-producing bark, hard wood and sawdust highly valued by the carpenter, the slow-growing oak, familiar in Europe and Asia, is unknown in Australia and tropical Africa. In various American forms, as the black, red, pin, white and swamp oak, it ennobles the forests of America in the north temperate zone. The familiar ashen-barked white oak was the frequently named land mark in old deeds.

86

Indian Knife. 242. The mosaic shows one of the small, acutely pointed triangles of jasper or flakable stone sharpened into chisel shape at the broad end, used by Indians unmounted for pocket knife, chisel, needle, punch and scraper.

Indian Pipe. 245. Having invented the process of smoking crumbled tobacco leaves, always largely mixed with osier cornel inner bark, or bearberry leaves, or other herbs, the Indian made tobacco pipes of clay, bonfire baked, or carved from the soapstone quarried along the Delaware or Potomac, or from the celebrated red pipestone or catlinite imported from the ancient Indian quarry in Missouri.

242

245

246

Grooved Indian Net Sinker. 246. A pebble e n c i r c l e d with a shallow groove, was tied by Indians to the fish net woven of cords twisted from Indian hemp (*Apocynum cannabium*) and other vegetable fibre, as a sinker.

Indian Making Fire. 249. Twirl the two-foot-long spindle, not twice as thick as a lead pencil (of cedar, buckeye, grease wood or slippery elm), upon the edge of the hearth stick, about a foot long or less, and two or more inches broad, (of cedar, pine, yucca or slippery elm), so that the charred dust thus frayed up by the twirling runs over the hearth's edge down a notch previously cut, upon some dry surface, and until the smoking dust pile glows with an internal spark. Then touch the ember with tree fungus, called punk, and blow the latter when aglow against vegetable fibre (arbor vitæ frayed and scorched, cedar, or inner birch bark) for a flame in from eight to fifty seconds. Make your first experiments in a museum with original fire sticks, tested and well dried, or your ill-chosen woods and tinder will fail you when you seek to master the primeval craft of the Lenni Lenape, Choctaw, Cherokee, Apache, Ute, Zuni, Shoshone, Bilhula or Klamath. The fire which it takes

249

the Aino of Japan thus an hour and a half to make, has been produced by the dexterous Pueblo in a few seconds. But when you thus twirl the potent spindle after the fashion of the Masked Priest in the Mayan Codex Trojano, get two or three friends to help you, seizing the fire stick by turns, and after throwing water on the wood, with united desperate effort, make, if you can, the sacred fire of Zuni.

Indian Stone Spade. 244. Having killed and dried a number of trees by "blazing" them, so as to admit sunlight into the forest,

244

the Indian corn planter scratched holes in the primeval loam, working either with sharp charred sticks, or flat stones about six inches wide and one inch thick, chipped into the form of spades as represented in the mosaic.

Indian Spear. 247. Certain early Spanish travelers having noted the use of spears by North American Indians, we may infer that many of the chipped stone blades longer than 2½ inches, and often found

247

277

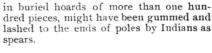

in buried hoards of more than one hundred pieces, might have been gummed and lashed to the ends of poles by Indians as spears.

The Linden. 277. (*Tilia americana.*) Tracing its ancestry to the fossil trees of Arctic tertiary times, the noble linden or bass wood, with its inner fibrous bark or bast fit for basket making, gave its name (line or lind for linden) to the celebrated Swedish botanist, Carl Linne, or as Latinized, *Linnaeus.* The massive noble tree, with its ruby winter buds and creamy summer flowers beloved by bees, with its large heartshaped leaves and dense shade, glorifies the Pennsylvanian forest.

The Black Bear. 252. (*Ursus americanus.*) With dog and gun, man finds a bloody amusement in rapidly exterminating the honey-loving, ant- fish- root-eating, vegetarian and carnivorous black bear. Glossy black, brown-cheeked, dog-fearing, harmless (unless with cubs or in self-defense), the tree-climbing, hibernating animal was reverenced, almost worshipped, yet hunted and eaten by Indians in the primeval forest. Close kin to the brown bear of Europe, the once abundant black bear in vain retires to inaccessible places to escape the relentless and untiring hatred of his human pursuer.

252

Mask of the Owl Man. 240. The mosaic illustrates one of the ceremonial, horrible, human masks, symbolizing ideas of birds, animals, reptiles, or the forces of nature, worn by Indian Priests and sometimes described by travelers, but rarely found by archæologists, as recently were many such in the wood-preserving mud of an East Florida swamp. The miniature wooden original, about three inches long, well carved and polished, with convex silver discs for eyes, was given to the family of its possessor by Tedyuscung, the Lenni Lenape Chief.

240

The Opossum. 254. (*Didelphys virginiana.*) Sluggish, easily caught, p e r s i m m o n-loving, prehensile-tailed, death-counterfeiting, related to the *marsupial* kangaroo of Australia, prolific, and carrying its four to twelve young in a breast pouch, the opossum, defying extermination by man, and hurting his human enemy by blood-sucking the latter's table chickens, is here represented as climbing through the branches of a tree.

254

253

The Linden. 253. (*Tilia americana.*) Tracing its ancestry to the fossil trees of Arctic tertiary times, the noble linden or basswood with its inner fibrous bark or bast fit for basket making, gave its name (line or lind for linden) to the celebrated Swedish botanist, Carl Linne, or as Latinized, *Linnaeus.* The massive noble tree, with its ruby winter buds and creamy summer flowers beloved by bees, with its large heartshaped leaves and dense shade, glorifies the Pennsylvanian forest.

Indian Making Spear Blades. 250. After the manner of most primitive peoples in the Stone Age, the Indian begins to make the stone blade by chipping a flakable mass of natural jasper as only he can chip it, into a leaf-shaped pattern, by means of hammering with a quartzite pebble. Seated near one of the natural outcrops of jasper in the Lehigh hills, the master craftsman, whether Delaware, Nanticoke, Iroquois or Susquehannock, until about the year 1650, with a skill never equaled by civilized peoples, made blades large or small, thin or thick, for use as arrow points, spearheads, knives, scrapers or perforators.

250

258

Sweet Gum. 258. (*Liquidambar styraciflua.*) The lofty, erect, sweet gum, with its burrlike, brown winter fruit, winglets of corky bark skewered through its branchlets like the scales of an alligator, called liquid-ambar and alligator wood, is not so resinous as its Asiatic cousins producing the storax gum. With its five-pointed leaves of unsurpassable beauty, it outvies the foliage of maple trees in the flaming glory of its autumn color.

Buttonwood. 251. (*Platanus occidentalis.*) The huge sycamore tree, seventy to one hundred feet high, with conspicuous scaly bark, is decorated over winter with brown button-shaped fruit. Massive limbed, with open shade, early bared in autumn, and with scaly bark glittering white green and gray along the river, the tree was the farmer's choice of old to shade the spring house.

Indian Grinding Corn. 266. In a stone dish hollowed by pecking with another stone, by means of the precious and laboriously made slim stone cylinder, the pestle, the Indian woman pulverized grains of maize, dry or fire parched, into a meal, mixable with mashed boiled pumpkins, beans or chestnuts, and baked, with dried venison or huckleberries, on a hot

251

266

269

stone, or in oak bark embers, thus originating the "johnny," "hoe" and "ash" cake of the imitative Virginia negro.

Arrowhead.

269. Although the irregular and eccentric unchipped stone flakes of the Easter Islanders and prehistoric Japanese were not known in America, there was a great variety of form in the points of Indian arrows, chief of which may be noted the barbed, as here shown, for lacerating a wound, and the unbarbed which would pull out easily.

Cherries. 146. (*Cerasus.*) Rival of the strawberry, beloved of boys and birds, associated with the flavor of cherry bounce and pie, the delicious European fruit, in its best known forms of pie, oxheart, or black cherry, when freshly imported, and grown by the log cabin of the pioneer, may have been seen by the Indian before his expulsion from Pennsylvania.

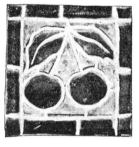

146

The Pennsylvanian must thank the horticulture of his European ancestors for this fair fruit of early summer, brought to Europe by Lucullus the Roman epicure, from Cerasus of Asiatic Pontus. Cultivated for centuries in France England and Germany, the cherry tree, if in Pennsylvania degenerating in fruit, has not failed in the magnificence of its white bloom, which, gladdening the roadsides when the meadow lark sings his spring song, only yields to those blossoms which the Japanese wonder at on April seventh.

256

Indian Picture of the Rattlesnake. 256. Not in America only but throughout the world, the serpent, hated, worshipped and feared, pervades in thought and shape the religious symbolism of primitive peoples. Here, it is the malignant head with open jaws, surrounded by a scaled coil of the deadly rattlesnake (*Crotalus horridus*), as scratched by a mound-building Indian upon a breast plate of shell, that the mosaic reproduces.

260

Indian Gorget. 260. One of the thin tablets of slate or shale, generally smooth and oblong, perforated with two holes, frequently found at Indian village sites, and in mounds; or when in graves, generally near the breast of the skeleton, and called gorgets, though the early travelers do not describe them in use.

Catalpa. 263. (*Catalpa catalpa.*) Native of the warmer forests of the Gulf States, transplanted from the South to the Pennsylvanian woods, the large-leaved, heavily white-flowered candle tree,

263

or Indian bean, or catalpa, as the Cherokees called it, has escaped from cultivation in the North, to scatter its winged seeds and shine with its white and purple-tinted flowers in shady woods and along the banks of streams.

Indian Corn. 255. Cultivated universally in the New World, protected from winter death by continual care, cooked by the Indians in many prehistoric ways not yet imitated, propagated far north of its Mexican birthplace, the world-wide, the prolific and super-nourishing maize (*Zea mays*) the beautiful, or Indian corn, achieves a popularity as great in the eyes of civilized as of savage man. Civilization may not thank the Indian for his great gift, but the discoverers brought maize in triumph to Spain, and because no European carved or painted design shows the plant before Columbus, because literature fails to mention it, this so-called *gukurutz* of Turkey, the *grano turko* of Italy, masking its American origin in Oriental names, testifies to the agriculture of the Indian. As excessively eaten by man in Lombardy (under the familiar name of polenta) and cause of the disease called pelegra, waving its green fronds in Turkey, gladdening the plains of Asia and the clearings of the Congo, whether indigenous to darkest Africa or not, the plant may justly be regarded as one of the Indian's greatest gifts to the civilized world.

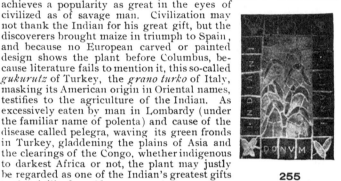

255

265

Indian Pipe. 265. The mosaic shows a remarkably worked black stone nearly a foot long, carved by Indians with immense pains for use as a tobacco pipe. The specimen, suggesting in form the tail of an eel, belongs to the large class of precolumbian Indian or Mound Builder pipes of clay or carved stone, made in animal and grotesque patterns or as straight tubes, and illustrating the origin of the now widespread habit of tobacco smoking by man. This class of pipes is easily distinguished from another class of small well burned clay pipes, often of Dutch make, and often found at Indian village sites, sold by Europeans (by about 1650) to the Indians, after the former had learned from the latter how to smoke tobacco and make pipes.

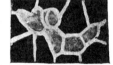

267

Indian Amulet. 267. Stones three or four inches long, carved into highly conventionalized forms of animals, reptiles, or very frequently birds, though not noticed in native use by early travelers, are continually found in Indian mounds and at village sites and called amulets for want of a better name.

231

Indian Hoeing Corn. 231. Sparsely grown or still barren and forest encompassed areas, called by farmers "Indian fields" in Pennsylvania, and still existing in original timber land, probably show aboriginal "clear-

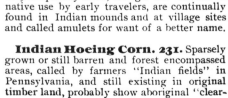

293

ings," where having destroyed trees by blazing, and hacked them down with stone axes after charring the trunks, the Indians planted corn. The mosaic shows an Indian woman digging around the growing maize plant with an unhafted stone hoe.

Arrowhead. 293. These stone points for the wooden shafts of the Indian's arrows, have been found in Pennsylvania almost everywhere, and constitute the chief relics of the stone age.

Indian Ceremonial Stone. 243.

Carved by Indians at immense pains by means of pecking, sand rubbing and polishing, and perforated with hollow reed drill and wet sand. A multitude of little stones, three or four inches long like this, found in ancient mounds and village sites, having been unnoticed and unexplained by early missionaries and travelers who might have observed them in use by the Indians, have been ignorantly called "ceremonial" stones by the modern archæologist.

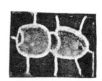

243

264

Indian Paddling Canoe. 264.

With skillful twisting stroke of the wooden paddle, the Indian propels his light, keelless, nail and pegless, equi-ended boat, made of large strips of the wonderful bark of the paper birch tree, (*Betula papyrifera*), sewn upon a wooden frame with root fibre threads, and gummed together.

The Banner Stone. 241.

Found in Indian village sites, graves and mounds, from three to six inches long, transversely pierced, and worked by pecking, grinding and rubbing into two wing like projections, the mysterious stone here represented, belongs to a type of relics of the vanished Indian and Mound Builder, frequently found, but not having been explained by observation of the early travelers, called Banner Stone for want of a better name.

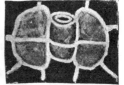

241

274

Indian Ceremonial Gorget. 274.

Thin tablet of shale or slate, generally perforated with two or more holes for suspension. Sometimes notched upon the edges but very rarely decorated. Frequently found in Pennsylvania at the sites of Indian villages, or when at Indian graves, close to the breast of the skeleton. The Lenape Stone found in Bucks County, inscribed with a rude picture representing the sun, moon, stars and lightning, and a conflict between Indians and the extinct hairy mammoth (*Elephas primigenius*), elaborately carved on its reverse with symbolic figures, inadequately studied or ignored by archæologists, outvies in archæological interest all such stones previously found.

271

Wolf. 271. (*Canis occidentalis.*) Hunting in winter packs, running down foxes and smaller animals, or destroying the larger disabled elk or moose, howling, burrowing, always hungry, tamed by savages, and part ancestor of the friendly dog, the American gray wolf, devourer of sick bison and bison calves and domestic cattle, has been more easily driven off and exterminated than his fierce cousin of northern Europe.

289

Indian Grooved Stone Axe.
289. The stone axes of prehistoric Europe were perforated for the insertion of handles. A few grooved hammers or axes of stone have been found in Italy, and they occur in Australia, but the American Indian seems peculiar in having universally made these implements and mounted them by binding with rawhide thongs, handles of wyths, or doubled or perforated sticks, around and about the grooves worked upon the stone.

276

Indian Pipe. 276. The mosaic shows a remarkably worked black stone carved by Indians with much pains for use as a tobacco pipe. The specimen belongs to the large class of precolumbian Indian or Mound Builder pipes of clay or carved stone, made sometimes in animal and grotesque patterns, or as straight tubes, and illustrates the origin of the now widespread habit of tobacco smoking by man. This class of pipes is easily distinguished from another class of small well burned clay pipes, often of Dutch make, and often found at Indian village sites, sold by Europeans (by about 1650) to the Indians, after the former had learned from the latter how to smoke tobacco and make pipes.

Heckewaelder Preaching to the Indians. 270.

270

The Moravian missionary, minister of Christ's p e a c e and brotherhood among Indians, venerable, noble, beloved, upholding a friendship for the red man equal to that proclaimed by Penn, but which long outlived the latter's transmutation into race hatred among the ruling colonists, here preaches to the Lenape, after a common fashion, standing upon a stump in the partly cleared woods.

Arrowhead. 275. The Indians sometimes pounded malleable native copper into arrowheads, but otherwise ignorant of metal working, they, like most primitive peoples, chipped flakable stones to suit their purpose. The gunflint makers of the last century, until recently surviving at Brandon in Sussex in England, working the flint with iron hammers, illustrate in a coarse and clumsy manner, the high skill of the prehistoric blade chipper, which no modern imitator has been able to equal.

Indian Making Dugout Canoe. 279.
Having felled by charring and hacking its base, a tree, the Indian seated astride the log, cuts out with a grooved stone axe the charred areas of successive fires built upon the wood and restricted by the appli-

275

279

cation of water and clay, into the desired hollow boat.

Indian Drill.
294. The mosaic shows one of the small narrow acute angled triangles of jasper or other flakable stone, sharpened at the broad end and anciently used by the Indians unhafted as pocket knife, needle, chisel, punch and scraper.

294

Indian Tubular Tobacco Pipe. 290.
Perforate a stone six to eight inches long at immense pains, by bow drilling it from both ends with a hollow reed helped by sand and water. Enlarge the hole at one end or both. Rub round and polish the whole tube, and you produce as the Indian produced it, one of the earliest forms of tobacco pipes, through which as seen in prehistoric manuscripts of Yucatan, the masked Indian priest in certain ceremonies blew the smoke of odoriferous herbs to the four world quarters.

290

Indian Shooting with the Bow and Arrow. 280.
A few primitive races of the world were probably ignorant of the bow as the great weapon of war and chase. The kneeling Indian propels a deadly point of chipped jasper (an arrowhead), lashed and glued to the end of a stick (the arrow), by the spring of a deer thong or gut drawn backward from a flexible stick (the bow); thus using the greatest of all war and hunting weapons ever developed by primitive man, yet unknown to the Australians who used the boomerang instead.

Grooved Indian Axe. 285.
The stone axes of prehistoric Europe were perforated for the insertion of handles. A few grooved hammers or axes of stone have been found in Italy and they occur in Australia, but the American Indian seems peculiar in having universally

280

made these implements and mounted them by binding with rawhide thongs, handles of withes, or doubled or perforated sticks, around and about the grooves worked upon the stone.

Catalpa. 288.
(*Catalpa catalpa.*) Native of the warmer forests of the Gulf States, transplanted from the South to the Pennsylvanian woods, the large-leaved, heavily white-flowered candle tree, or Indian bean, or catalpa as the

285

288

Cherokees called it, has escaped from cultivation in the North, to scatter its winged seeds and shine with its white and purple tinted flowers in shady woods and along the banks of streams.

Indian Smoking Tobacco.

281. (*Nicotiana tabacum.*) In small doses and always combined with a large proportion of aromatic leaves such as those of the bearberry, or the fine dried and powdered inner bark of the osier cornel (*Cornus stolonifera*), or other herbs, but never pure, the Indian smoked the dried leaves of tobacco. (*Nicotiana tabacum.*) If the Chinese did not indirectly learn the strange art, from the Indians' immemorial practice, the latter certainly through Nicot, Hawkins and Raleigh, taught it to Spain, France, England, Holland and Germany, and even to the conservative Mohammedan, who did not mention the practice in "The Thousand and One Nights."

Indian Ceremonial Stone.

286. Carved by Indians at immense pains by means of pecking, sand rubbing and polishing, and perforated with hollow reed drill and wet sand. A multitude of little stones

281

three or four inches long like this, found in ancient mounds and village sites, having been unnoticed and unexplained by early missionaries and travelers who might have observed them in use by Indians, have been

286

ignorantly called ceremonial stones by the modern archæologist.

Redbud. 288. (*Cercis canadensis.*) Where a wild vanguard of southern redbud or Judas trees grow in the Susquehanna woods, stand beneath the yet leafless boughs gleaming in crimson blossoms, and while the bees hum and the spring zephyr brings memories of the far away southern forests, forget even the snowy shad bush and the white vernal glory of the matchless dogwood.

Indian Ceremonial Stone.

272. Thin tablet of shale or slate, generally perforated with two or more holes for suspension, sometimes notched upon the edges, but very rarely decorated. Frequently found in Pennsylvania at

288

the sites of Indian villages, or when at Indian graves, close to the breast of the skeleton. The Lenape stone found in Bucks County, inscribed with a rude picture representing the sun, moon, stars, and lightning, and a conflict between Indians and the extinct hairy mammoth (*Elephas primigenius*), and elaborately carved on its reverse side with symbolic figures, in-

272

adequately studied or ignored by archæologists, outvies in-archæological interest all such stones previously found.

The Spider. 278. Type of nature's mystic power, first instructor of man in weaving, aërial rope-maker, sinister, in-domitable, potent, transmitter of the primeval fire of the Cher-okee across the "World Water" on his gossamer web, the spider encircled by the lines of his masterful skein is here shown as carved by an Indian upon a brooch of shell.

278

Massacre of Friendly

Indians by Whites. 298. William Penn is long since dead, and his friendship for the Indian transmuted in-to a tide of race hatred which the pious Moravian strives in vain to stem. Then in 1763 a Scotch-Irish band of borderers known as the Paxton Boys, shocked the colony by murdering at Conestoga and in Lancaster Jail several defenseless Con-estoga Indians, Christianized by the Moravians.

298

Triangular Indian Arrowhead. 283. Out of about one hundred typical forms of chipped stone arrowheads, produced by the aboriginal in-habitants of the new world from Behring Straits to Patagonia, one of the conspicuous shapes is that of the acute angled triangle, frequently found in eastern Pennsylvania and rare if not unknown to prehistoric Europe.

283

Arrowhead. 295. The Indians sometimes pounded malleable native copper into arrowheads, but otherwise ignorant of metal working, they like most primitive peoples, chipped flakable stones to suit their purpose.

The Elm. 291. (*Ulmus americana.*) Less conspicuous and beloved for village shade than in New England, the American white or water elm of Pennsylvania, often vase shaped in the outline of its plumed branches, loves water courses and escapes the barbarism of Pennsylvania German village tree-topping, in moist woods. The most noted tree of its kind in Pennsyl-vania, venerated as shading the celebrated treaty of Penn with the Indians at Ken-sington in 1682, and protected from fire-wood hunters by the British General Sim-coe's sentry in the Revolution, blew down in 1810 at an age of 283 years.

295

291

Indian Pipe. 282. Having invented the process of smoking crumbled tobacco leaves, always largely mixed with osier cornel inner bark or bearberry leaves or other herbs, the Indian made for the purpose pipes of clay and baked them in bonfires, or pipes carved from the soapstone quarried along the Delaware or Potomac, or cut from the celebrated red pipe-stone or catlinite imported from the ancient Indian quarry in Missouri.

282

Indian Celt. 284. Though the grooved stone axe of the ancient Americans is generally unknown in prehistoric Europe, the celt, a wedge-shaped stone implement six inches or more long, formed by pecking and polishing, gummed and tied transeversely or longitudinally with withe or raw hide into its handle of wood, or held loose in the human hand, was common to both hemispheres, and served the savage of ancient America or Europe as knife, scraper, chisel, wedge, hatchet, gouge, crusher and grinder.

284

Arrowhead. 296. The ancient Egyptians and Scandinavians and the Mexicans, possessing fine grained flint or volcanic glass called obsidian, were probably more skillful in the art of stone blade chipping than the northern Indians of eastern North America, who were seen to produce their stone blades in various ways: by percussion, by flaking with pebble hammers, by leverage, or by direct pressure with deer antlers or bone points.

296

Spearhead. 297. Many large leaf-shaped stone blades were mounted on short wooden handles as knives, and many were u s e d un-mounted; others again, as the illustrations of early Spanish explorers show, were fastened upon the ends of poles and used as spears by Indians

297

Pine Cones. 292. Represented by about 39 related species in the United States, shallow rooted, evergreen, highly valued for its white wood distilled for turpentine and pitch, darkening the Rocky Mountain slopes or sandy seacoast, whispering in varied æolian tones, and as the white pine (*Pinus strobus*) rivalling in beauty the cedar of Lebanon or the deodar of India, the pine tree rapidly destroyed by American axe and movable saw, awaits its last chance of preservation as a tree domesticated for ornament.

292

Indian Rock Picture. 340. Man, bird or demon, made probably by Delaware, Iroquois or Susquehannock Indians, by pecking with sharp hard stones upon the face of a large water-worn boulder known as Big Indian Rock, in mid-Susquehanna at Safe Harbor, cut near a group of thunderbirds, symbolic eagles, animals,

340

bird tracks and a human head, on the east face of the rock.

Quail. 319. (*Ortyx virginianus.*) Prolific, ground-nesting, non-migratory, gathering in winter coveys, preserved by game laws, rising for the sportsman with explosive whirring of wings, cheering summer with his lively "bobwhite" note how did the now meadow-loving quail subsist in the earlier days of the great meadowless forests?

319

Indian Brooch Inscribed With a Cross Symbol. 322. Whether derived from thoughts of the four points of direction, from primitive exorcisms, from the worship of reproductive forces or otherwise, the cross used as a symbolic decorative form far antedating the discovery of America by Columbus, is sometimes shown in the handiwork of the native Indian. Here the mosaic reproduces the native design scratched upon a shell gorget.

Wild Cat. 321. (*Lynx rufus.*) Yellowish brown, short tailed, with hair tufts on ears, spotted with dark brown or black, scaring its prey with a wild scream, sleeping in hollow trees, caves or rock shelters, destroying young birds in the nest, mincing catnip, wallowing in strong scented herbs, stalking rabbits and grouse in the twilight of dawn or eve, unearthing mice or watching at squirrel holes, the wild cat springs from ambush or overhead bough upon his larger prey. This relative of the domestic cat, lion, tiger, leopard, and fossil

322

American sabre-toothed smilodon, has been driven by his old enemy the Pennsylvanian farmer to the few remaining forest fastnesses of the Alleghenies.

The River of Fire. 273. The iridescent scum floating on the furface of Oil Creek, long afterwards precious as petroleum, then soaked up by the savage as a lotion, is here set on fire by Indians in the seventeenth century, according to an old account, in honor of a visit of Canadian Jesuit priests, who stand upon the bank admiring the spectacle.

321

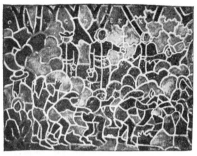

273

Indian Quarrying Jasper. 323. With crow bar made of a young tree burned down, charred at the end, and hacked to a point with a stone axe, the Indian quarryman pries a mass of jasper, cracked by fire, from the native ledge, as at Durham in Bucks County, at Macungie, and at Vera Cruz in Lehigh County with its 250 prehistoric digg ngs, where he thus worked at the bottom of pits eighteen feet deep.

Red Fox. 336. (*Vulpes fulvus.*) Sly, stealthy, slit-eyed, night hunting, cleanly, devourer of birds, chickens, mice, moles, squirrels, fish, beetles, or fruit, less swift than his European cousin, whether as the red fox of the north or the grey fox of the south, the celebrated animal, either burrowing in the earth or living in rocks and hollow trees, is respected and hated by man. Driven into nets or dug out for extermination until about 1650 in Britain, the fox began to alure the red-coated hunter and his hounds by the end of the 17th century. Thenceforward, partially protected as a target for sport, glorified by his destroyer in the fun of pictures, horns, hounds, redcoats, Irish reels, club rooms and balls, he becomes the type of the national sport of England transferred to America.

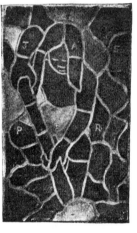

323

336

The Raccoon. 337. (*Procyon lotor.*) Cousin to the bear, hibernating in winter, feeding on shellfish, mussels, birds, turtle eggs, insects, nuts, fruits, frogs and corn, soaking its food in water, this gray-brown animal with white-striped tail, dwelling in trees, hunting at night, and a good swimmer, is easily tamable as a pet by man, who has not exterminated him in Pennsylvania.

Bullfrog. 343. (*Rana catesbiana.*) Prolific, laying thousands of eggs in warm water, which pass from tadpole to frog in early summer days, making summer nights echo with his deep bellowing, feeding upon insects, snails and reptiles, the bullfrog has rathe increased than diminished in numbers

337

since the destruction of the great forest.

Indian Symbol of the Human Head. 339.

343

As a probable representation of the head of a man with protruding scalp lock, the mosaic shows one of the many figures, here in outline but generally in full intaglio, pecked by Indians with hard sharp stones on the east face of Big Indian Rock in the Susquehanna rapids at Safe Harbor.

339

The Muskrat. 350.

(*Fiber zibethicus.*) The amphibious prolific muskrat, inhabiting lakes and streams, invading cultivated lands, threatening dams and canals, destroying the waterlily and lotus where they had flourished before, defies man's effort to dig him out and exterminate him, and increases rather than disappears before the same civiliza-

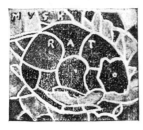

350

tion which, in exterminating the bloodletting mink which had filled the muskrats' galleries with blood in the past, has withdrawn from the life struggle the muskrat's worst enemy.

Indian Drawing of the Spider. 330.

Aërial rope-maker and weaver, poisonous, indomitable, potent, the spider has commanded the venerating attention of the savage. Here the mosaic reproduces a drawing by the Indian who, conventionalizing the outline of the insect with great skill, scratches it upon the concave face of a shell, used as a breast plate or gorget.

White Children Rescued by Indians. 335.

For a time Penn's roseate dream of loving brotherhood between European and savage, typified

330

by the famous treaty of the great elm, seemed realized. Not yet overreached by the land purchase known as the Indian Walk, still uninjured, unangered, unsuspecting, the red men with no wrongs to revenge, mingled kindly with the foreigner. Early in the eighteenth century, two little white children named

335

325

Chapman, lost in the forest near Wrightstown, Bucks County, were kindly rescued by Indians and restored to their distressed parents.

Primitive Tobacco Smoking. 325. Not probably until in ceremonies and exorcisms, the smoke of odoriferous herbs had thus been blown by Indian priests to the four world quarters through tubes of stone or clay, would soporific tobacco be preferred to other plants, or as *kinnikinnick*, when mixed with bearberry leaves or osier cornel under bark, be smoked for pleasure by the Indian inventor of smoking.

Treaty Wampum Belt. 327. Great belt of purple black and white shell-beads, representing an Indian shaking hands with a hatted European, reasonably believed to have been given to Wil-

liam Penn by the Lenni Lenape Indians, at the famous treaty under the elm tree at Shackamaxon (the Kensington north suburb of Philadelphia), in 1682. Several thousand multi-colored fragments of unio or clam shell, about one-quarter inch in diameter and one-half inch long, were longitudinally pierced by Indians at great pains with stone

327

or bone drills. More precious than gold to the red man as "wampum," "peg," "slawant," "beak," or "ronoak," sometimes passing as money on strings, or used as seals to solemnize the acts of men, or at animal sacrifices, and as symbolic of war (where white meant faith, black meant battle, and red meant blood), in the form of beads, they were strung on vegetable fibre threads interwoven with animal thongs so as to form a belt.

347

Locust. 347. (*Cicada septem decim.*) With summer song as familiar to the country boy as the "knee-deep" of frogs in early spring, hatched from twig deposited eggs to crawl downwards antlike into the ground, buried for seventeen years or less as an eyeless grub, the misnamed insect is related to many varieties of cicada (not locust) in the old and new world, but neither to the grasshopperlike insect of the biblical Egyptian plague, the pest of modern north Africa, nor to the food eaten by St. John the Baptist.

Rattlesnake. 338. (*Crotalus horridus.*) Less poisonous than the cobra of India, or the fer de lance of Martinique, devourer of small rodents, the deadly rattlesnake where he survives in the Appalachians from New Hampshire to Florida, is justly dreaded by man.

338

(**338** Continued)
About four feet long, sluggish, coiling, rattling, reluctantly striking, the brown or blackish yellow diaper-striped snake was avoided and venerated by Indians and white men, and but very rarely conciliated by snake loving mountaineers who dare to pick up the fanged reptile in their hands.

Wild Turkey. 320.

(*Meleagris gallopavo.*) While the colonist and farmer readily gives a place in the farm yard to the domesticated turkey, tamed for him by ancient Mexicans and cliff-dwelling Indians, he rapidly exterminates the wild bird which Franklin had wished to use as a national emblem. A native of America, the domestic turkey called Welsch Hahn in Germany, spread into Europe so soon after Columbus's discovery as to be painted in the barn yard scenes of Italy, by the painter Bassano early in the sixteenth century.

Rattlesnake as Pictured by Indians. 324. The head

with open mouth of the fearful rattlesnake (*Crotalus horridus*), surrounded by a coil of the scaly body ending in

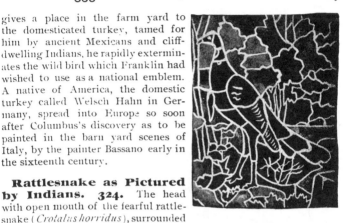

320

its rattle, highly conventionalized after the manner of other designs found in Indian mounds, and upon wooden masks excavated in Florida. The mosaic here reproduces a carving deeply scratched upon a breast plate of shell by the mound building Indians.

Indian Rock Carving.

334. One of nearly 200 other animal figures, probably a bear, pecked with a sharp stone by Indians against the side of Little Indian Rock in the Susquehanna rapids at Safe Harbor.

324

334

Tortoise. 328. Celebrated in

white man's story and legend, venerated as an emblem of wisdom by the Indian, the sluggish unwieldy reptile, heavily armored above and below by carapace and plastron, resists without much effort the attack of many

328

318

enemies; sometimes defying the tearing of the eagle's beak and talons as when, if legend be true, a bird of prey high in the air, killed the Greek poet Aeschylus by dropping a tortoise upon his head.

The Blue Jay. 318. (*Cyanura cristata.*) The trumpet cry of the blue jay startles the quiet woods while his wings flash azure through the leaf shadows, as upon his omnivorous search for food he seizes the autumnal chestnut, or in spring devours young birds and steals bird eggs, no less remorselessly than the ornithologist multiplies his skins for the cabinet, or the lady distorts his blue stuffed form, glass eyed, upon her hat.

The Hawk or Eagle. 329. Represented by many species, caricatured by the bird stuffer, "taken" and retaken by the ornithologist, nailed to the barnside by the farmer who hates him, the hawk or his eagle brother was yet admiringly adopted as a national emblem by aristocrat, king and democrat, stamped upon the "almighty dollar," and glorified in stone carvings by the savage Indian as the genius of thunder. Devourer of birds, frogs, rodents and reptiles, and of the flesh foods appropriated by man, soaring above clouds in mastery of the gift of flight, darting like lightning upon his prey, the wonderful bird, less wary than the crow, proclaims by his existence a victory hard won in a never ending struggle with his human enemy.

329

Indian Basket Maker. 326. Only less important to primitive man than the plastic clay utensil, is the basket as here plaited by an Indian woman in one of many masterful plaits. Sometimes watertight, decorated with conventionalized and artistically balanced patterns, the Indian basket was usually superior in make and decoration to the wares of civilized peoples.

326

Indian Rock Carving. 299. One of the animal figures, probably a panther, pecked by Indians by pounding with a sharp stone against the smooth, freshet-worn, eastern side of a large boulder known as Big Indian Rock, in the middle of the rapids of the Susquehanna at Safe Harbor.

Porcupine. 349. (*Erethizon dorsatus.*) The largest carnivore hardly

299

349

(**349** Continued)
dares attack the irritating ball of arrows which constitutes the bristling defensive armor of the porcupine, who by a slash of the tail may defeat his attacking enemy with a suddenly injected mouth-paralyzing volley of his sometimes deadly barbed quills. Tree climbing, greedy of salt, devouring the inner bark of elm, basswood and hemlock trees for food, the non-hibernating animal who nests in a hollow tree, was hunted by Indians for food and for his quills valued as decorations for moccasin, belt and pouch.

Indian Rock Picture. 344.
Thunderbird with Forked Tail. One of about twenty figures of men, animals and their tracks, reptiles, birds and demonic symbols, pecked with stones by Indians upon the sides of Big Indian Rock, near the much more profusely inscribed fellow boulder, Little Indian Rock, in mid-Susquehanna at Safe Harbor. The grinding of driftwood in freshets slowly erases these wierd and sinister symbols of a vanished race, placed in the midst of roaring and dangerous rapids.

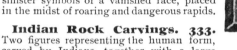

Indian Rock Carvings. 333.
Two figures representing the human form, carved by Indians, together with a large

344

number of pictures of animals, birds and their tracks, and reptiles, upon the faces of two large boulders known as Big and Little Indian Rocks, in the middle of the rapids of the Susquehanna at Safe Harbor.

333

The Crow. 237. (*Corvus americanus.*) Not from his striking color and figure, his anatomy or his habits, according to the bird book, might the non-migrating, incomparably sagacious, grain-eating crow claim distinction, but rather from the fact that he stands supreme among birds as victorious in an eternal life struggle against the human maxim, man-condemned but man-practiced, that might makes right. Marshalled in destructive flocks, guided, guarded and generalled, scouting, watching, venturing, despising the scare-crow, evading trap and poison, guaging gun range as it extends, the ever-present crow, defying the northern winter, despoils the human

237

spoiler from the exact standpoint of the latter.

345

The Weasel. 345.
(*Putorius vulgaris.*) Sometimes turning all white in winter, brown-backed, keen-

scented, night-hunting, wholesale destroyer and blood-sucker of rats, mice, moles, frogs, birds and chickens.

Indian Brooch Inscribed with a Cross Symbol. 331.
Here the mosaic reproduces a native design scratched upon a gorget or breast plate of mussel shell. Whether it is derived from the four points of direction, from primitive demon worship, or from ceremonies based upon the blowing of the winds, the handiwork of the Indian, produced at a time antedating the discovery of America by Columbus, sometimes to the great surprise of early travelers, showed as in the case illustrated, the pattern of the Christian Cross.

331

Rattlesnake as Pictured by Indians. 332. The
head with open mouth of the fearful rattlesnake (*Crotalus horridus*), surrounded by a coil of the scaly body ending in its rattle, highly conventionalized after the manner of other designs found in Indian mounds, and upon wooden masks excavated in Florida. The mosaic here reproduces a carving deeply scratched upon a breast plate of shell by the mound building Indians.

332

Oak Leaves. 1. Long
lived, colossal, durable, highly valued for wood, bark and sawdust, represented by a multitude of varieties, as

red, black, swamp, willow, chestnut and pin oak, or as the familiar ashen-barked white oak frequently marking the land boundaries in old deeds, the oak though unknown in Australia and tropical Africa, ennobles the forests of Europe, Asia and America in the north temperate zone.

The Log House. 4.
Build a rectangle of heavy logs

1

as in the mosaic, notched at the ends to fit closely, with wattled chimney smeared with clay. Saw out doors and windows and roof with bark or shingles handsplit with frow and club. Caulk with grass and clay and you have the original house of the settler, copied from ancient forest houses in Europe. Still built in wild regions of the Appalachians and the west, and surviving eastward as landmarks recalling a vanished human past as forcibly as do the ruined castles of Europe.

4

Sour Gum. 3. (*Nyssa sylvatica*.) The mosaic shows the leaves of the sour gum tree familiar in northern and southern States as the pepperidge and tupelo. Lofty, tough, fine-leaved, flashing scarlet in autumn, and heavily fruited with blue berries once beloved of the now vanished wild pigeon and other birds. Often the hollow trunked harbor of "coon" and "possum," the tree furnished cylindrical hollow trunk sections which sometimes lined the spring to make the water "taste sweet," or stood in the old orchard or barn as "bee-gum" (beehive) or "salt gum" (salt box) for cattle feed.

The Axe and Its Ancestor. 2. The American pioneer having brought with him from England, France or Germany, the long bitted (bladed) short polled axe of his ancestors (to the left in the mosaic), soon put the previously little used instrument to immense and unheard of use in forest felling, and after 1730 modified the wabbling tool into a more square, compact, and effective wedge, by weighting and enlarging the poll or driving part, and shortening and lightening the cutting wedge or blade. Thus the country blacksmith after 1730 produced a "pitching" (tree felling) axe indigenous to the United States, (to the

right in the mosaic), and unknown except by American exportation, in other countries where as against the overbalancing American poll, the bits or blades of old world axes always outweigh their polls.

Felling the Forest. 5. Neither steam car, trolley, automobile, coal or iron mine oil or gas well, probably worked the terrestrial change suddenly produced when the white colonist with resounding blows of the long-bitted axes of his ancestors, first dissipated the immemorial tree shade of the great forest. The ancient red American retired or perished. As houses, cities and villages rose, the chimney swallow nested in its first chimney, the purple martin in its first man-made toy-house, and the wren in a man-prepared calabash. The quail and lark left the forest for open fields of man-planted grass, and the crow first robbed the farmer's corn. The prolific muskrat liberated by farmer's trap from his mink enemy overpopulated the banks of mill ponds. The housefly first buzzed in the log horse-stable, and the European house rat overran the region, while the watercress of the old world invaded springs newly sunlit, and a hundred new European flowers sprang up by freshly cleared roads.

8

Hickory. 8. (*Hicoria ovata.*)
Among the pignut, mocker and
bitter nut family of hickories, is
the lofty shellbark with its delicate
nuts prized and stored by Indians
and white men, with its immense,
combustible, long-burning bark
scales, furnishing the fockle or fishing torch of the rural fisherman,
and the similar night light of the
cave exploring Indian, who has
scattered the floor of Wyandotte
cave in Indiana with the burnt ends
of his hickory bark torches. The
celebrated shellbark tree famed for
its elastic wood, furnished to the
pioneer the axe handles, first
straight, later curved, which gave
spring to the deadly stroke of his
forest-destroying axe.

Red-Eyed Vireo. 7.
(*Vireo olivaceus.*) One of the
tireless little songsters, feeding on
insects, staining his white throat
with pokeberries, blackberries and
mulberries, and devoted foster parent to the foundling cowbird.

7

6

Orchard Oriole. 6. (*Icterus spurius.*)
Where the red earthen pots dry on fence
palings, where the buttonwood tree overhangs
the spring, or where by the old smoke house the
west wind scatters apple blossoms, the orchard
oriole richly feathered in orange and black hangs
his swinging nest; and the question arises how
and where did he live and love when orchards
did not exist, when the vast sun darkening forest
shadow was everywhere, and when no bird's eye
had yet seen the life of the farm.

Pioneer Rifleman. 9. A marksman of deadly aim from
continual shooting at Indians and animals, the Pennsylvanian pioneer,
armed at first with a transatlantic gun, barreled with spiral bore to
make the flying leaden bullet rotate, (Edward Marshall the Indian
walker's rifle 1737-50 made at Rothenburg, Germany) began making
his own "Lancaster" and "Kentucky" rifles at Reading, Lancaster,
and elsewhere, by the end of the 18th century. Though subject to
speedy annihilation in a bayonet charge, and denied a place in
European armies by Napoleon, or-
ganized bands of these deadly, slow-
firing, Indian fighters, with raccoon
caps, buckskin shirts, and fringed
leggings, did great service in frontier
battles and at New Orleans, in 1815,
where the riflemen lying behind
cotton bales and supplied by boys
with continually reloaded extra rifles,
destroyed at a distance the British
Army, killed its general, and won the
battle in a few minutes.

9

Grey Squirrel. 12. (*Sciurus
carolinensis.*) Having survived the

(**12** Continued)

12

enmity of the farmer who shoots and eats the squirrel or imprisons him in a tin cage and treadmill, the animal finds peace in the city park and town grove, where city children tame and feed him.

Shovel Plow. 11. After a very ancient model minus plowshare and mould board, surviving from Roman times and still used for plowing out potatoes. The settler scratched newly cleared land with whamight be called the blade of a shovel fast tened vertically to a plow frame (the shovel plow), thus tearing the fibrous tangle, shallow or deep, or skipping it, while escaping upset with easy plow jumps, where the coulter of a normal plow might lock under roots.

Beaver. 10. (*Castor fiber.*) While the prolific subterranean muskrat delivered from his terrible enemy the mink, multiplies in the midst of civilization, the sensitive beaver instantly shrinks from contact with the human invader who has almost exterminated him in Pennsylvania. The story of his matchless skill becomes a half-forgotten school

11

boy's fable, and common knowledge no longer testifies to the fact that the animal resembling an enormous heavy-tailed muskrat, gnaws down trees so as to lock them across streams, thereby forming driftwood dams with sufficient water for his island village.

Bee-Hive. 16. A small dome-shaped straw basket about eighteen inches high, made of spiral rye straw strands, string-bound and perforated midway with wooden skewers, upon which the bees built their comb, was constructed, together with the more primitive hives of hollow logs, as a bee house, by the Pennsylvanian colonist who finding no honeybees in pre-columbian America, brought with him the honeybee from Europe. These yellow domes gleaming under the apple trees of the Pennsylvanian farm, or as pictured upon the State shield of Utah, seen in use in Bucks county in 1897, and for sale at Chester, England, in 1900, necessitated through lack of extra honey compartment the cruel drugging, often killing of the bees with sulphur smoke, to get the honey.

10

16

Reaping With the Sickle.

13. Lean forward and seizing a large bunch of wheat or rye with the left hand, cut the stalks near the ground by drawing the keen serrated narrow sickle blade across them from left to right. Then as the mosaic shows, you reap as your ancestors did from Egyptian times until about 1820, when at the advent of the European grain cradle, or the Hainault scythe (dispensing with stalk grasping), and

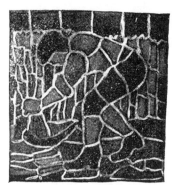

13

(**13** Continued)

finally the reaping machine, the greatest craft of husbandry changed suddenly and forever.

Song Sparrow. 14.

(*Melospiza melodia.*) Below the ripples where the mill stream lingers by bridge or eddy, and where the jetty water beetles dart upon the odoriferous pool, the song sparrow, seizing a branch of hazel or the topmost fresh-leaved spray of willow, outvieing all his kindred, stirs the heart with his sweetest keynote of spring.

The Dutch Scythe. 17.

Holding the instrument by its much twisted handle, you stoop little as you mow with the ancestral scythe of Germany, now 1908 superseded in Pennsylvania by the Anglo-American hard steel so-called English scythe. To sharpen the Dutch scythe, hammer (dengle) thin with the dengle hammer, its broad malleable blade held close with the left hand upon a wrought iron wedge-shaped little anvil (ambus) driven into a log or stump. Then whet the scythe with a sandstone whetstone soaked in vinegar, carried in a cow's horn

14

hooked at your leathern belt. Thus came of old the familiar evening noise of tinkling hammers (dengeln), where·the breeze scented with new-mown hay drew through the slatted corncrib, where by hanging saw and pig's grease, the axe wedged the log, and the worn grindstone and wood-horse rested on the fragrant chip floor of the ancient wood-house.

Sour Gum. 20. (*Nyssa sylvatica.*)

The mosaic shows the leaves of the sour gum tree, familiar in northern and southern states as the pepperidge and tupelo. Lofty, tough, fine-leaved, flashing scarlet in autumn, heavily fruited with blue

17

berries once beloved of the now vanished wild pigeon and other birds, often the hollow-trunked harbor of "coon" and "possum," the gum tree furnished cylindrical hollow trunk sections which sometimes lined the spring to make the water "taste sweet" or stood in the old orchard or barn as "bee-gum" (beehive) or "salt gum" (salt box) for cattle feed.

19

20

Cardinal Bird. 19. (*Cardinalis cardinalis.*)

Crested, vivid scarlet, heavy-billed, active,

nonmigratory, named from the scarlet robe of the Catholic high priest, most conspicuous of songsters, lurking in summer in chosen wet bramble thickets, or flashing hope and warmth into the drab woods of winter, the cardinal bird, rich in song, is often seen imprisoned for life in a small cage.

Baltimore Oriole. 18.

(*Icterus galbula.*) Gleaming black and orange through the summer boughs of hickory, apple, oak and maple, named indirectly after the Irish town Baltimore through

the heraldic colors of Lord Baltimore founder of Maryland, destroyer of insects, brilliant musician, migrating in winter to Mexico, the magnificent "hanging" bird in nest building gladly seizes upon once unknown strings, rags and lint of the modern white American, minus which the oriole must have built his hanging pouch-like nest of vegetable fibre and twigs, in the shadows of the great forest, with greater trouble than now where the swaying maple boughs welcome him by the farm or spring house.

18

Sharpening the Dutch Scythe. 21.

The broad malleable blade of the Dutch scythe "Dengle sense" of ancient German pattern, was hammered sharp upon an iron wedge anvil driven into a stump. The farmer then whetted it with a vinegar-soaked sandstone hone carried in a cow's horn hooked to his belt. On the other hand the hard steel English scythe, which now supersedes the German instrument, is never hammered and only whetted.

21

Shellbark Hickory. 15.

(*Hicoria ovata.*) Among the pignut, mocker, and bitternut family of hickories, the lofty shellbark with its delicate nuts prized and stored by Indians and white men, with its immense combustible, long burning bark scales, furnished the fockle or fishing torch of the rural fisherman, and the similar night light of the cave exploring Indian who has scattered the floor of Wyandotte cave in Indiana with the burnt ends of his hickory bark torches. The celebrated shellbark tree, famed for its elastic wood, furnished to the pioneer the axe handles, first straight, later curved,

15

which gave spring to the deadly stroke of his forest destroying axe.

Scarlet Tanager. 23.

(*Piranga erythromelas.*) One man in a thousand, carefully listening while the robins are singing, recognizes the mellow reedlike notes of the tanager in the high oak grove. The kindlier twentieth century student or egg-hunting boy, looking skyward where the young leaves

23

tremble in the zephyrs of spring, sees daylight through the bird's loosely woven nest holding blue eggs spotted with purple. But every eye must see, every voice exclaim, when the magnificent tanager, in intense scarlet, black-winged and black-tailed, flashes his tropical splendor against the green world of early summer.

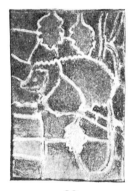

Opossum. 22. (*Didelphis virginiana.*) Sluggish, sleepy, helpless, death-feigning, fruit, insect, and chicken-eating, hunted and eaten with delight by the American, slave and free, continually caught and killed by the farmer, the celebrated, prolific, American marsupial, ghastly in hair and skin, unknown in Europe, and related to the Australian kangaroo, continuing to rear about thirty-six young per year, in three litters, in its extraordinary breast pouch, survives its human enemy, and still harbors unsuspected close to the farmer's henroost and haystack or in his hollow apple tree.

Indian Walk. 25. So as to buy from the Delaware Indians, by agreement with Richard and Thomas Penn, as

22

much new land as a man could go over in a day and a half, Edward Marshall, in 1737, starting at a chestnut tree in Wrightstown, Bucks county, walked or ran, by way of a previously blazed path, to the neighborhood of Mauch Chunk, including by a surveyor's ruse, (to the disgust of the Indians), an enormous unexpected tract for the Buyers, in the required time. The Indians refusing to vacate the land and being driven out by intrigue, revenged themselves afterwards upon Marshall and his family and upon Pennsylvania thirty-nine years later at the massacre of Wyoming.

25

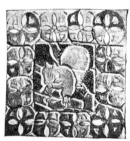

Grey Squirrel. 28. (*Sciurus carolinensis.*) Having survived the enmity of the farmer, who shoots and eats the squirrel, or imprisons him in a tin cage and treadmill, the animal finds peace in the city park and town grove, where city children tame and feed him.

Catbird. 27. (*Galeoscoptes carolinensis.*) The slate-colored, black-polled

28

catbird, haunting blackberry bushes, thickets and shrubbery, eating raspberries, strawberries, blackberries, mulberries, cherries, grapes, spice and pokeberries, nesting with four greenish-blue unspotted eggs in a heavy twig nest, is familiar near the Pennsylvanian farmhouse and orchard from April to November. One hundred persons know well the mewing catlike note of the bird to one who recognizes his full enthusi-

27

astic May song varied with imitations of other bird notes.

Swamp Blackbird. 26.

26

(*Agelaius phœniceus.*) Lovable and never to be forgotten, the dramatic swamp blackbird, with jet-black uniform shoulder strapped in fiery scarlet, rivals the gay butterfly in the sunbeams of swampy meadows, as by bulrush, wild rose and calamus, clutching the reed stalk, he sounds his mellow love call to the summer wind.

Blowing the Dinner Horn. 29.

A little before noon, while the steam of boiling pot and frying pan rises from the kitchen fire, stand without the door, and blow by lip vibration, a straight mouthpieced tin horn about five feet long. The far reaching sound calls the farmer to dinner from the fields. Disused in Eastern Pennsylvania about 1840. Its older rival the conch shell (*Strombus gigas*) still (1908) blown to open lock by canal boatmen on the Delaware and Lehigh Canal, and was blown to call to dinner in Buckingham, Bucks county, in 1897. Like the two former horns, the cow's horn, still sold (1907) in Charleston, South Carolina, for foxhunting, was also sounded by vibration of the lips.

29

Shellbark Hickory. 32.

32

(*Hicoria ovata.*) Among the pignut, mocker, and bitter nut family of hickories, the lofty shellbark, with its delicate nuts prized and stored by Indians and white men, with its immense, combustible, long-burning bark scales, furnished the fockle or fishing torch of the rural fisherman, and the similar night light of the cave-exploring Indian (who has scattered the floor of Wyandotte cave in Indiana with the burnt ends of his hickory bark torches). The celebrated shellbark tree, famed for its elastic wood, furnished to the pioneer the axe handles, first straight, later curved, which gave spring to the deadly stroke of his forest destroying axe.

Sour Gum. 30.

30

(*Nyssa sylvatica.*) The mosaic shows the leaves of the sour gum tree familiar in northern and southern states as the pepperidge and tupelo. Lofty, tough, fine-leaved, flashing scarlet in autumn, heavily fruited with blue berries once beloved of the now vanished wild pigeon and other birds, often the hollow-trunked harbor of "coon" and "possum," the gum tree furnished cylindrical hollow trunk sections which often lined the spring to make the water "taste sweet," or stood in the old orchard or barn as "bee-gum" (beehive) or "salt gum" (salt box) for cattle feed.

Red-Headed Woodpecker.

31. (*Melanerpes erythrocephalus.*) You must search among the painted birds of the tropics for a rival to this magnificent insect hunter, who startles the silent woods with sudden resonant drumming upon dead tree limbs, or darting in red black and white through summer leafage, protests in his thrilling life, against the farmer who would shoot him because he eats cherries, the untaught boy who destroys him for fun, or the woman who wears his distorted skin or wings upon her hat.

31

Gristmill. 33.

Grain-grinding by random blows or rubs of stone upon stone or wood, was succeeded by the quern mill, namely an ancient hand mill in which a stone disk, perforated in its centre for the insertion of grain, and pivoted upon a larger rimmed disk beneath it, was made to revolve on the latter by a handle inserted near the circumference. As the primeval food-producing flour mill of Christendom, the quern survives in remote parts of Europe, and as a paint grinder (1897) among Pennsylvania German potters. Enlarged querns ground by wind or water, dating from remote European antiquity, formed the flour and grist mills of Eastern Pennsylvania until, upon the introduction about 1890 of the Austrian method of squeezing and crushing the grains, between various sized rollers equipped with sieves, grain came to be ground in cities and the roadside mill yielded to the factory.

33

The Red-Headed Woodpecker. 36.

(*Melanerpes erythrocephalus.*) The sight of the brilliant bird with scarlet head, white breast and wings, and black body, gamboling upon the old "worm fence," drumming upon the dead tree top, or startling the woods with cheerful trumpet, might well recompense advancing humanity for all the corn and apples that the bird may eat between his insect feasts.

36

Grey Squirrel. 35.

(*Sciurus carolinensis.*) Having survived the enmity of the farmer who shoots and eats the squirrel or imprisons him in a tin cage and treadmill, the animal finds peace in the city park and town grove, where city children tame and feed him.

Robin. 34.

(*Merula migratoria.*) A few boys in the year 1908 begin to feel that when on the fairest morn of May, the redbreast perched among apple blossoms, wafts his love song upon the spring breeze, the sight and sound are worth all the cherries the bird may afterwards eat. But an older human generation had to be influenced to cease robin killing by opening the insect-filled stomach of the

35

Left Corridor.

(**34** Continued)

34

songster to reassure that of the man. Robins eat insects and insects eat fruit, therefore robins help man to eat more fruit.

Spinning Flax. 37. The flax fibre after being cleaned and dusted from the stalk, *broken* and *scutched*, and scratched into strings, *hetcheled*, is wound into a lump upon a forked stick, the *distaff*, from which the woman draws and forms it with her right hand, feeding it with her left fingers, upon the whirling *spindle* which further twists and spools it into threads

coarse or fine, for the subsequent home weaving of shirts, towels, under and outer clothing and household linen. Slowly developed in Europe from an Asiatic original by the 17th century, brought thence by colonists to America, and discontinued about 1820 to '40, this once all important, omnipresent footrun machine, antedating the factory, and announcing woman's work, was probably preceded here as in Europe by the primeval hand distaff and spindle whorl which still survives in remote corners of the world.

37

Wild Duck. 40. Everywhere pursued by sportsmen, represented by many species whether nesting in Pennsylvania or the far north, migrating at railroad speed high in the air, in Y-shaped flocks, lured by wooden decoys, stalked from blinds, retrieved when dying in the water, by so-called Chesapeake Bay dogs bred from a Labrador original in 1807, courting death or danger whenever in season he lights for food or rest on pond, river or bay, the wild duck out classes in the typical form of the celery-eating canvasback, all lauded products of the American kitchen.

40

Sour Gum. 39. (*Nyssa sylvatica.*) The mosaic shows the leaves of the sour gum tree, familiar in northern and southern states as the pepperidge and tupelo. Lofty, tough, fine-leaved, flashing scarlet in autumn, heavily fruited with blue berries once beloved of the now vanished wild pigeon and other birds, often the hollow-trunked harbor of "coon" and "possum," the gum tree furnished cylindrical hollow trunk sections which often lined the spring to make the water "taste sweet," or stood in the old orchard or barn as "bee gum" (beehive) or "salt gum" (salt box) for cattle feed.

39

Tin Lantern. 38. A conical-roofed cylinder of tin plate, with handle ring and candle socket, and without glass windows or reflector, was the universal farm lantern of the Eastern United States, and well known in England and Ireland, from the early eighteenth century until about 1840. A similar form, probably of brass, used in

38

(**38** Continued)

the middle ages, but not common till the invention of tin plate in England in 1670 made the tin lantern possible. Lights and shadows flicker through its punctured glass-less sides as through the brazen network of the mosque lamps of the Mohammedan orient. Hide the tin lantern under your coat on the way to the barn on a windy night or out it goes. Seen in use at Connellsville in Fayette County in 1890.

Catbird. 43. (*Galeoscoptes carolinensis.*) The slate-colored, black-polled cat-bird, haunting blackberry bushes, thickets and shrubbery, eating raspberries, straw-berries, blackberries, mulberries, cherries, grapes, spice and pokeberries, nesting with four greenish-blue unspotted eggs in a heavy twig nest, is familiar near the Pennsylvanian farmhouse and orchard from April to No-vember. One hundred persons know well the mewing catlike note of the bird, to one, who recognizes his full enthusiastic May song varied with imitations of other bird notes.

Clearing the Forest. 42. The mosaic shows in Latin, the words LABOR VINCIT SYLVAM Translated—Labor conquers the for-est, referring to the work of thous-ands of human hands, in felling that part of the primeval forest named after William Penn, in rolling and burning logs and brush, in digging out roots, and in plowing and plant-ing the virgin earth. Thus it hap-pens that particles of charcoal can

43

be found in nearly every square foot of Pennsylvanian soil.

42

Orchard Oriole. 41. (*Icterus spurius.*) Where the red earthen pots dry on fence palings, where the button-wood tree overhangs the spring, or where by the old smokehouse, the west wind scatters apple blossoms, the or-chard oriole, richly feathered in orange and black, hangs his swinging nest; and the question arises, how and where did he live and love when orchards did not exist, when the vast sun-darkening forest shadow was everywhere, and when no bird's eye had yet seen the the life of the farm?

Chimney Swallow. 46. (*Chætura pelagica.*) Continually on the wing, moving at the rate of a mile a minute, skimming the pond's brim, dipping under water, or darting close to the meadow grass, master in

46   **41**

the matchless gift of flight, the short-tailed, long-winged, dusky, chimney swallow must have ceased gluing his nest of twigs to the walls of caves and hollow trees, and resorted to the previously unknown farmhouse chimneys, about 1720. When (1860-'90) the farmer substituted a small stone flue for the old chimney, or capped the latter with a terra cotta tube, the bird turned (1880) to the houses of the rich, where large chimneys were revived.

45

The Elk. 45. (*Cervus canadensis.*) Yellow-bodied, with brown head and mane, an immense deer, with huge antlers shed and regrown yearly, wallowing in mud, or standing in water to escape summer flies, herding in season, called "Wapiti" by the Iroquois Indians, and miscalled elk by whites, the animal is glorified in scores of geographical names upon the American map. He was exterminated by sportsmen and gunners in Pennsylvania about 1850.

Hawk. 44. With secret admiration, the farmer nails to his barn side the feathered carcass of the fierce, soaring chicken robber, his master in the supreme physical gift of flight, demonstrating by continued existence, the bird's victory in a never ending struggle with the human gunner. Cousin to the eagle, one of a race admired more than the gentler lower creatures, by patriots, statesmen, legislatures, kings, aristocrats and democrats, the bird typifies strangely the unchristian aspirations of democratic America, republican France, autocratic Russia, and imperial Germany and Austria, stamping now the "almighty dollar" with patriotic suggestion, as it once called to duty the legions of Rome or the warriors of Napoleon.

44

Splitting Shingles. 47. Before the days of lumber mills, sections of oak logs

were split into shingles by pounding with a club, upon an L-shaped knife, the frow Then a man sitting astride a homemade device, the shaving horse, and clamping the shingles by foot pressure upon a lever, trimmed and smoothed them with a drawing knife.

47

Oak Leaves. 53. Long lived, colossal, durable, highly valued for wood, bark and sawdust, represented by a multitude of varieties, as the red, black, swamp, willow, chestnut and pin oaks, or as the familiar ashen-barked white oak, frequently marking the land boundaries in old deeds, the oak, though unknown in Australia and tropical Africa, ennobles the forests of Europe, Asia and America in the north temperate zone.

53

Cardinal Bird. 49. (*Cardinalis cardinalis.*) Vivid scarlet, crested, heavy-billed, active, nonmi-

(**49** Continued)

gratory, named from the scarlet robe of the Catholic high priest, most conspicuous of songsters, lurking in summer in chosen wet bramble thickets, or flashing hope and warmth into the drab woods of winter, the cardinal bird, rich in song, is often seen imprisoned for life in a small cage.

49

The Red-Headed Woodpecker.

48. (*Melanerpes erythrocephalus.*) The sight of the brilliant bird, with scarlet head, white breast and wings, and black body, gamboling upon the old "worm fence," drumming upon the dead tree top, or startling the woods with cheerful trumpet, is worth in inspiration to advancing humanity, all the corn and apples that the woodpecker may eat between his insect feasts.

48

Sour Gum. 57. (*Nyssa sylvatica.*) The mosaic shows the leaves of the sour gum tree, familiar in northern and southern states as the pepperidge and tupelo. Lofty, tough, fine-leaved, flashing scarlet in autumn, heavily fruited with blue berries once beloved of the now vanished wild pigeon and other birds, often the hollow-trunked harbor of "coon" and "possum," the gum tree furnished cylindrical hollow trunk sections which often lined the spring to make the water "taste sweet," or stood in the old orchard or barn, as "bee-gum" (bee-hive) or "salt gum" (salt-box) for cattle feed.

57

Woman Dipping Candles.

52. From a small six eight or ten-armed turnstile, the woman lifts off the suspended wooden disks, one by one, each hung with from twelve to thirty candle wicks, and immerses the wicks in tallow, melted over water in a large pot swung upon a wood fire. Where the autumnal wind blows cool by the sooty smokehouse or flagged out-kitchen, the grease hardens into candles as the disks go round.

Red-Eyed Vireo. 50. (*Vireo olivaceus.*) One of the tireless little songsters, feeding on insects, staining his white throat with pokeberries, black-

52

50

berries and mulberries, and devoted foster parent to the foundling cowbird.

Redbud. 56. (*Cercis canadensis.*) Where a wild vanguard of southern redbud or Judas trees grow in the Susque-

56

(**56** Continued)

hanna woods, stand beneath the yet leafless boughs gleaming in crimson blossoms, and while the bees hum, and the spring zephyr brings memories of far away southern forests, forget even the snowy shad bush, and the white vernal glory of the matchless dogwood.

Thrashing With the Flail.

55. After (in Roman times) the thrashing of grain by cattle-tread, by rolling of logs, or by the scratching of boards toothed with flint chips, the flail, a short staff swung upon a long one, invented in the middle ages, followed the pounding out of grain with a single stick. The flail in 1900 survived on small Pennsylvanian farms, where the rythmic strokes of several thrashers together, drummed the barn floor like the hoof echoes of a trotting horse upon a hard road.

Sugar Maple. 54. (*Acer saccharum.*)

In none of its variously named forms of swamp, rock, red, silver, or transatlantic Norway, is the maple family so renowned as in the celebrated tree with warped bark ribs, known as the sugar maple (*Acer saccharum.*)

55

Having perforated the bark with small holes, under-drained with little sheet iron troughs, catch the exuding sap in buckets, to be boiled and hardened as maple sugar, or liquified as maple syrup, nationally renowned as a sweetening for the hot buttered buckwheat or griddle cake.

54

Screech Owl. 51. (*Megascops asio.*)

Red or grey, with feathered hornlike ears, feeding upon mice, beetles, moles, grasshoppers and small birds, nesting with four or five nearly round white eggs in a hollow tree, the screech owl, finding food and shelter where he may, remains over winter in Pennsylvania. Long after the milkers' lanterns have left the barn, and early risers have gone to bed, before the late April moon rises, and when all is silent at the farm save for the nightly stamp of the stabled horse, or the splash of falling water in the log trough, the quavering sinister hoot of the screech owl, frightens the wakened slumberer with a world-old fear.

Cooking Apple Butter. 58.

After paring and cutting the apples, boil down the pieces in cider all night.

51

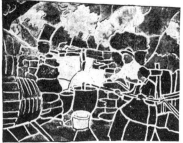

58

(**58** Continued)

Let the whole able family stir by turn, with the perforated arm of a pole, as the mosaic shows, or with a cranked paddle, reducing the liquid to the consistency of a dark brown thick sauce. Thus you make the famous *laht varreck* or apple butter of the Pennsylvania German, derived from the less universal *latwerge* (fruit sauce) of Germany.

The Oak. (Without number.) Long lived, colossal, durable, highly valued for wood,

bark and sawdust, represented by a multitude of varieties, as the red, black, swamp, willow, chestnut and pin oak, or as the familiar ashen-barked white oak, frequently marking the land boundaries in old deeds, the oak, though unknown in Australia and tropical Africa, ennobles the forests of Europe, Asia and America in the north temperate zone.

The Spud. 62. With a small concave blade at the end of an iron

(**Without Number**)

rod hafted in a wooden handle, you push under and peel off the bark of the rock, black, swamp and chestnut oak, or best of all, of the birch tree, for use in tanneries. This work now confined to lumber regions, or zones of tree-extermination by steam saws, was once common on eastern farms, while tree felling was still universal, and domestic tanneries now extinct, always in need of bark, followed the sound of the axe.

Plowing With the Shovel Plow. 61. The plowman skips, scratches, or deeply furrows the newly cleared land, where among stumps and fibres a plowshare would wedge under horizontal roots. Thus

62

he works with a plow, armed with a shovel-shaped, nearly vertical blade, still used in 1908 to turn out potatoes, and surviving through the middle ages from a Roman original.

Stove Plate. 60. The mosaic shows the pattern of one of the five-plated iron "wall" or "jamb" stoves (1720-1760) made to heat not cook, of five heavy cast-iron plates without stovepipe or door. Like a box the ancient

61

60

(**60** Continued)

stove protruded into the room it heated, and being fed by fuel inserted into it through a wall hole, emitted its smoke through the same orifice and backward into an adjoining fireplace. Here under the name of the iron master and a series of symbolic tulips, and above the date 1751, is the motto "DAS. LEBEN. JESU. WAS. EIN. LICHT." Translated—The life of Jesus what a light.

Catching Terrapin. 63.

Thrust an iron-pronged pole into the deep cold mud at the brook's eddy, until a dull vibration tells you of the self-buried carapace of the fresh water terrapin, asleep for the winter. Then pull him out with a spoon-shaped fork on the reverse of the pole, and bag him. Thus the catcher exterminates rapidly, for sale at about three dollars per dozen, the fresh water terrapin (*Pseudomys rugosa*), to resell as meat of his famous edible cousin, the salt water terrapin (*Malacoclemmys palustris*), at five dollars per quart.

Sour Gum. 65. (*Nyssa sylvatica.*)

The mosaic shows the leaves of the sour gum tree, familiar in northern and southern states as the pepperidge and tupelo. Lofty, tough, fine-leaved, flashing scarlet

63

in autumn, heavily fruited with blue berries once beloved of the now vanished wild pigeon and other birds, often the hollow-trunked harbor of "coon" and "possum," the gum tree furnished cylindrical hollow trunk sections which often lined the spring to make the water "taste sweet," or stood in the old orchard or barn as "bee-gum" (bee-hive) or "salt-gum" (salt-box) for cattle feed.

65

Lard Lamp. 64.

The characteristic lamp of the world from Roman times until the 19th century, and generally used in farms, cabins and mills in Pennsylvania until 1820-'40. Easily traceable backward through the people's lamps of Italy, Germany, Russia, Turkey, France, the Azores, Spain and Scandinavia, to ancient times. Of sheet or wrought iron, brass, tin or copper, boat-shaped like the double-trayed croosie of Scotland, or the synagogue lamp of Morocco, with long barbed and sometimes swiveled hook, the lamp was frequently adorned upon its hinged or pivoted lid, with a handle shaped after the chicken cock, in memory, like many vanes (in shape) and water spigots (in name), of the turning of St. Peter at the cock's crowing. Thrust

64

the hooked prong into a beam, or catch its barb on a nail or log
crevice. Then filling the vessel with lard (kept liquid in cold weather
with a hot brick), liquid animal fat, linseed or whale oil, light the
twisted tow (later cotton) wick, laid along the lateral trough and so
tilted as to allow the oil oozing from the flame to flow back into the
lamp. By the light brighter than a candle, read after dark, work
at the loom, or paint and varnish with vegetable colors and cherry
gum liquified in whiskey, the "Fractur" manuscript. Thus in Oc-
tober 1897 David Getter fried potatoes at night on the open hearth of
his log cabin near Springtown, Bucks county, Pennsylvania.

Frying in the Open Fire. 68. Reaching a long-handled
wrought iron pan, greased with lard or ham fat, over the glowing oak

or hickory embers of the kitchen
hearth, the farmer's wife fried
"saus," ham, puddings, mush,
scrapple, fish, all meats indeed,
and pancakes, tossing the latter up
the chimney to turn and catch
them upside down. Disused with
open fire cooking 1830-'50.

Paring Apples. 67. Turning a small crank which causes a
skewered apple to revolve, you
make the apple skin fly off in a
long spiral as you press a spade-
shaped, strap-fastened knife to the
whirling fruit. Thus working in
Pennsylvania until about 1860, you
anticipated the modern apple paring
machine, and prepared the fruit for
the neighborly "schnitzen" frolic,

68

when a score of merry neighbors
cut up the pared apples to be boiled in
cider for apple butter. Before country
steam mills superseded the practice, songs
were sung in English, not German, among
Pennsylvania Germans, who having abol-
ished secular singing long ago, are at last
1908 perforce by the phonograph, strangely
introduced to the ignoble song tune of the
city concert hall.

Wild Duck. 66. Everywhere pursued by sportsmen, represented by many
species whether nesting in Pennsylvania
or the far north, migrating at railroad
speed high in air, in Y-shaped flocks,
lured by wooden decoys, stalked from
blinds, retrieved when dying in the water
by so-called Chesapeake bay dogs bred
from a Labrador original in 1807, courting

67

death or danger whenever in season he
lights for food or rest on pond, river, or
bay, the wild duck out classes in the
typical form of the celery fed canvasback, all lauded products of the American
kitchen.

Song Sparrow. 70. (*Melospiza
melodia.*) Below the ripples where the
mill stream lingers by bridge or eddy,
and the jetty water beetles dart in circles
over the odoriferous pool, the song
sparrow, seizing a branch of hazel, or

66

(**70** Continued)

the topmost fresh-leaved spray of willow, outvieing all his kindred, stirs the heart with his sweetest keynote of spring.

Candlestick. 69. A tube of sheet iron set upon a circular convex base, and provided with a movable socket raised or lowered in a slot, held the dipped or moulded candle, universal in the kitchen and farmhouse before the introduction of kerosene. Thereafter used by farmers to scrape off the bristles from the scalded carcasses of hogs.

70

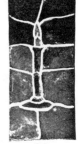

69

Fluid Lamp. 82. In this obsolete, short-lived pewter or glass lamp, with one, two or three small round wicks, the cradle light of many a man yet alive, and greatly in vogue between 1840 and '50, burned the so-called camphine, a fluid mixture of turpentine and alcohol. Keep the tube capped while not in use to save evaporation. If you lose the little pewter cap generally chained to the wick tube, replace it with a cock's spur.

82

Pounding Hominy. 81. Break and hull the grains of corn in a heavy wooden mortar hollowed from the trunk of a gum tree, by pounding with a bar of smith-forged iron, or a wood-hafted iron wedge. Thus the colonial farmer worked in Pennsylvania to prepare corn grains for subsequent boiling as hominy. Thus until 1880 negroes pounded hominy at Cambridge, Maryland. The colonial slave worked on a larger scale, as shown in the mosaic, with a heavier mortar and ponderous pestle suspended from the overbent springing top of a hickory sapling.

81

Tinder Box. 80. Holding between the thumb and forefinger of the right hand a piece of imported gun flint (long quarried at Brandon

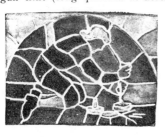

80

in Suffolk, England), strike it diagonally against a circlet of properly tempered steel held in the left hand, so that a spark flies downward upon a dry scorched linen rag lying in a tin cup (the tinder box). When the spark instantly catches the rag, blow or touch it into a flame against the sulphur-tipped end of a match which will not otherwise ignite. Then with the burning match, light a candle socketed in the lid of the tinder box, and smother the smouldering rag with an inner tin lid dropped upon it. Thus you were master of the house of a winter's morning when the fires were out.

This was better than spinning a wheel against a flint fixed at the end of a steel trough, or pounding fire upon tinder by air compression through a metal cylinder (1815–1820), or snapping a flintlock-tinder pistol. Disused with other light striking processes upon the invention of percussion matches about 1830.

Massacre of Wyoming. 78. The Lenni Lenape (Delaware) Indians having been cheated in their opinion out of their old Delaware Valley home, by the Pennsylvanian colonists at the "Indian walk" treaty in 1737, revenged themselves in 1776 as leaders of a British raid, by capturing "Forty Fort" at Wyoming, and killing and scalping their defeated enemies and neighboring settlers.

78

The Carpenter's Hatchet. 71. Two tools, the little hand axe and the claw hammer, served the carpenter until about 1800, to cut and pound wood, and to drive and pull wrought nails. When lath and plaster replaced ceiling beam, and wall panel, the hitherto unknown and incessant lath cutting and nailing required the invention of the American carpenter's hatchet

71

with an inferior side-notched nail pull upon the blade, which transformed the two older tools into one.

Husking Corn. 72. No machine having yet been invented to husk maize, the farmer having thrown the unbound shock of stalks, cleared from the "horse" stiffened stack, up n the ground, still (1908) kneels in the cold autumnal days, as his colonial ancestor did, upon the dry stalks, tearing the husk from the ear by means of a peg of

72

iron or wood, strapped to the mid fingers of the right hand, and projecting between thumb and forefinger.

Stove Plate. 73. The mosaic shows the pattern of one of the five-plated iron "wall" or "jamb" stoves (1720-1760) made to heat, not cook, of five heavy cast-iron plates, without stovepipe or door. Like a box, the ancient stove protruded into the room it heated, and fed by fuel inserted into it through a wall hole, emitted its smoke through the same orifice, and backward into an adjoining fireplace. Here under the name of the iron master and a series of symbolic tulips

73

74

and above the date 1751, is the motto "DAS. LEBEN. JESU. WAS. EIN. LICHT." Translated. The life of Jesus what a light.

Kingfisher. 74. (*Ceryle alcyon.*) The man with country boyhood, who learned to swim where still water runs deep in the "horse hole," or by the roaring breast of the old mill dam, can never forget the echoing trumpet of the kingfisher, as the restless, big-headed, black-collared bird, flying over the ripples and diving by pond lily, arum and calamus, sets going the wild echoes of woods, air and water.

Swingling Flax. 75. With the swingle or scutching knife (schwenk messer), a flattened club about 16 inches long of oak, the man knocks off loosened stalk shreds from the previously broken flax, held by handfuls across the end of an upright board. Disused 1830-'40.

75

Locust. 103. (*Cicada septem decim.*) The hot July air thrills with the song of the cicada (improperly called locust after the European grasshopper-like

103

insect), sounding his abdominal drum, who having come out of the earth (in extra hosts on certain years), climbs a few feet up a tree trunk, emerges from his translucent subterranean armor and takes wing.

102

Making the Farm Fence. 102. Three or four split and sharpened rails inserted into perforated hewn posts, superseded slowly the "worm" or "snake" fence made of split rails and poles piled zig-zag, or supplemented the wall fence of loose or mortared stones where stones were plenty.

100

Dragon Fly. 100. Believed to be the "doctor" or feeder of the water snake, by the barefooted country boy, as the latter searches the brook for bullfrogs, or lifts with skilled hand the unresisting half-hypnotized mullet "sucker" from his water hole under the bank. The dragon fly "snake feeder," emerging from an early submarine life, to cast its shell and take wing vies with the butterfly as a charmer of children, and type of the fire, and energy of mid-summer.

Making Bricks. 77. The red-shirted, sun-browned brickmaker, scattering sand and splashing water, slams a mass of soft plastic clay into a brick-shaped sanded mould of wood or iron, open at top and bottom. This when so filled, the barefooted "off-bearer" seizes, carries off to dump on the clay drying floor, and brings back empty. Generally disused (1895) for the mechanical process of squeezing plastic clay slowly through a brick-shaped tube, and cutting off into bricks with wire.

77

Medicine Mortar and Pestle. 76. The apothecary's assistant pounded drugs in a white marble mortar with a stone, wood or porcelain pestle, thus justifying the device of a mortar and pestle carved in wood and often gilded, symbolizing the art of medicine, still (1908) sometimes set above the pharmacy door as a sign. The mosaic, intended to express Pennsylvania's distinction in medicine, shows the Latin motto GLORIA CIVITATIS. Translated—Glory of the state.

76

Bat. 98. (*Vespertilio.*) Marvelous, weird, night-seeing, alert after a day trance, hanging heads downward on wing claws, in cave, hollow tree, open cellar, or ruined barn, sometimes for mother love weighted on the wing with clinging brood, the fantastic bats enter after dark the open window of the shining bedroom, snuff the kitchen candle, chase twilight beetles over tree top and lawn, or as demons of the night breeze, tease the boy players of "kick-the-wicket" who once followed them shouting as in the old Maryland child's rhyme—

98

"Leather-winged bat, fly under my hat
And I'll give you a ham of bacon."

Penn's Treaty. 97. As a noble-hearted leader of Christian Friends, seeking to mollify the stern rule of might makes right, by which advanced nations seize the waste lands of the world from their primitive owners, and by which Pennsylvania was granted him by the English Crown, William Penn desired to dispossess his Indian land owners by gifts and kindness rather than by force. To his honor and glory stands the memory of a celebrated treaty of friendship (broken afterwards in 1737 by his sons) with the Indian land owners, said to have been made by Penn under a large elm tree on the right Delaware River bank at Kensington above Philadelphia. In the midst of wharves, factories, ware-houses and a few ancient,

97

(**97** Continued)

smoke-blackened dwellings, a small marble monument now (1909) marks the site where the "treaty tree," protected by the British garrison in 1776 as a venerable relic, blew down in 1810 at the age of 283 years.

Heron. 79. Of many kinds, long-legged, deliberate in flight, fish-eating, wading in mud and water, nesting in colonies on small tree tops, migrating in winter to the south, often magnificently plumed in blue, white or green, and inadequately protected by bird laws, the unfortunate heron is still sacrificed (1909) in great numbers, and, in spite of twenty years of Audubon societies, indignation meetings, bird lectures and leaflets, killed by women's agents for head or hat decoration.

Cider Flagon. 106. A large wooden flagon, hooped and lidded, brought up cider from the cellar of a Saturday night, or in early apple season carried refreshment to the thirsty reapers, who toiled with grain cradle or sickle at wheat, rye or oats harvest, before the days of the reaping machine.

106

79

Bear Trap. 83. The little steel trap of to-day, used by boys to catch musk-rats, reproduces the form of the large blacksmith-made apparatus, whose toothed jaws fly together at touch of spring, to clasp in deadly grip the leg, tail or muzzle, of wolf, bear, wild-cat, porcupine or other large wild animal.

Gridiron. 84. Not over the flame of an evil-smelling, modern kerosene stove, nor under the gas jets of the modern city hotel range, nor over the anthracite coal fire of an unlidded stove, but close above the glowing hickory embers of the old open hearth fire, hold the chop, steak or fish, upon a wrought iron grill sometimes furnished with channeled bars. Then as distinguished from penetrating the

83

meat with hot water (boiling), penetrating it with hot fat (frying), penetrating it slowly with heated air in a confined oven (baking), or slowly with heated air radiated sideways from an open fire (roasting), you suddenly sear the meat in the uprising heat, so as best to retain its flavor and juices, (broiling). Thus in the simplest and most scientific manner, you cook a dish to set before a king. Now, coal oil and gas cook stoves, permitting to the cook many idle makeshifts, have changed cookery. "Roast beef" being nearly always baked, no

84

(84 Continued) longer really exists, and the country cook who often soaks potatoes after boiling, to the consistency of soap or beeswax, having cast aside the gridiron, frequently boils the beefsteak or mutton chop in hot grease, that is to say, fries it.

Quail. 85. (*Colinus virginianus.*) Prolific, ground-nesting, nonmigratory, gathering in winter coveys, preserved by game laws, rising for the sportsman with explosive whirring of wings, cheering summer with his lively "bob-white" note, how did the now meadow-loving quail subsist in the earlier days of the great meadowless forest?

85

Domestic Turkey. 88. The familiar farmyard turkey of Christmas and Thanksgiving feasts in America, having been originally domesticated from its wild Mexican cousin (*Meleagris mexicana*), by prehistoric New Mexican cliff dwellers and Aztecs, went first to Europe with the Spaniards. Bred in the farmyards of Italy, England, Germany and France, and illustrated in the paintings of Bassano in the 16th century, the American turkey, called "welsch hahn" and "indianer" in Germany, "dandon" in France, and miscalled after the Sultan's country in the land of its origin, came back to the new world by way of the old.

88

The Butterfly. 92. Through one of the most marvelous changes in nature, sometimes lasting over winter, by way of egg laid upon a twig, voracious leaf-eating skin-molting caterpillar, pseudo-death as a grub-mummy wrapped in self-made coffin, long sleep, and resurrection, the sun-loving, honey-seeking, gorgeous butterfly, canceling in winged beauty the caterpillar's harm, emerges upon the lap of summer to outvie the fairest of her flowers.

92

House-Fly. 94. (*Musca domestica.*) The familiar, buzzing, warmth-loving, house-infesting, disease-spreading insect, grown in filth and garbage, particularly horse manure and decaying fruit, and

94

developed within a month through egg maggot and fly, was probably introduced from Europe with the horse, by the first settlers.

Conestoga Wagon. 96. The immense ponderous schooner-shaped wagon, of probable German descent, named from the site of its earliest make along the Conestoga Creek in Lancaster county, with home-spun linen cover stretched on wooden bows, and drawn by four to six walking horses often equipped with bells, transported freight across the Alleghenies and south of New England lines of sea and lake transport, before railroads were built. In lighter form, a celebrated wagon of national type, as

96

the "prairie schooner," it bore the American emigrant and his family "Westward Ho."

Pine Cones. 99. Sawed for boards, hard or soft, yellow or white, or scored for exuding resin, covering the northern hills and southern swamps, origin of pitch, the pine tree, in various forms, but most distinctive as the beautiful white pine (*Pinus strobus*), with its bare wing-like limbs feathered only at the ends, rivals in form the cedar of Lebanon or the deodar of India. Cut with the axe or movable saw, and floated down the stream in the form of trimmed logs, the tree seems to approach extermination.

99

Milking the Cow. 89. Universally important in the economy of the American farm, of inestimable assistance to man as contributor for several thousand years, of beef, leather and milk, the cow everywhere proclaims the dependence upon European ancestry of the American, who having never domesticated and almost exterminated his own cow (the bison), utilizes the European animal domesticated by his prehistoric ancestors in the stone age.

89

Cherries. 110. (*Prunus cerasus.*) Rival of the strawberry, beloved of boys and birds, associated with the flavor of cherry bounce and pie, the delicious European fruit, in its best known forms

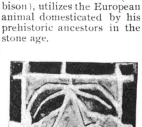

110

of pie, oxheart, or black cherry, when freshly imported, and grown by the log cabin of the pioneer, may have been seen by the Indian before his expulsion from Pennsylvania.　The Pennsylvanian must thank the horticulture of his European ancestors for this fair fruit of

early summer, brought to Europe by Lucullus the Roman epicure, from Cerasus of Asiatic Pontus. Cultivated for centuries in France, England and Germany, the cherry tree, if in Pennsylvania degenerating in fruit, has not failed in the magnificence of its white bloom, which, gladdening the roadsides when the meadow lark sings his spring song, only yields to those blossoms which the Japanese wonder at on April seventh.

Pressing Steel Plate. 123. The modern iron-worker flattens a sheet of hot steel by subjecting it to immense pressure under an hydraulic press.

123

Snapping Turtle. 186. (*Chelydra serpentina.*) Ferocious, carnivorous, devourer of frogs, tadpoles, and young ducks, only half-

protected by his under shell, always fighting in self-defense, most active of the turtle tribe in Pennsylvania, inhabiting the muddy bottom of the mill pond, the snapping turtle, grand trophy of torchlight fisherman and wandering boy, sometimes caught with red flannel on a fishhook, is the origin of a celebrated "snapper soup" popular in country restaurants.

186

Washington Crossing the Delaware. 90. On Christmas night 1776, General Washington led the American army secretly in flatboats, across the Delaware River just above the present (1908) bridge at Morrisville, Bucks county, and surprising the Hessian army employed by the British, defeated them at Trenton and captured their General Rahl.

90

Black Bear. 95. (*Ursus americanus.*) With dog and gun, man finds a bloody amusement in rapidly exterminating the honey-loving, ant, fish, and root-eating, vegetarian and carnivorous, black bear. Glossy-black, brown-cheeked, dog-fearing, harmless (unless with cubs or in self-defense), the tree-climbing, hibernating animal, was reverenced, almost worshipped, yet hunted and eaten by Indians, in the

95

primeval forest. Close kin to the brown bear of Europe, the once abundant black bear in vain retires to inaccessible places to escape the relentless and untiring hatred of his human pursuer.

109

With a round-bladed bark chisel, working like the man in the mosaic, the farmer stripped rock, black, swamp and chestnut oak bark, or best of all birch bark, for the tanner. Discontinued as a common practice with the abandonment of country tanneries about 1860.

Pine Cones. 119.

Sawed for boards, hard or soft, yellow or white, or

scored for exuding resin, covering the northern hills and southern swamps, origin of pitch, the pine tree, in various forms, but most distinctive as the beautiful white pine (*Pinus strobus*), rivals the cedar of Lebanon or the deodar of India, with its bare wing-like limbs feathered only at the ends. Cut with the axe or movable saw, and floated down the stream in the form of trimmed logs, the tree seems to approach extermination.

119

120

Flax Brake. 120.

An apparatus of heavy oaken home make. Three horizontal oak knives connect cross beams on legs. Hinged over them, two similar knives, weighted by heavy oaken ends and a parallel bar handle, dovetail between the lower knives at

each blow of the upper frame, which the worker lifts and drops with a down thrust upon the rotted flax stalks laid across. This reduces the useless stalk to fine splinters and chaff, which by a later operation, scutching or swingling, is dusted away from the fibre. Discontinued 1840-'60.

Oak Leaves. 124.

(*Quercus.*) Long-lived, colossal, durable, with color-producing bark, hard wood and sawdust, highly valued by the carpenter, the slow growing oak, though familiar

124

in Europe and Asia, is unknown in Australia and tropical Africa. In various forms, as the black, red, pin, white, and swamp oak, it enno-

bles the forests of America in the north temperate zone. The familiar ashen-barked white oak was the frequently named land mark in old deeds.

The Elk. 91. (*Cervus cana-densis.*) Yellow-bodied, with brown head and mane, an immense deer, with huge antlers shed and regrown yearly, wallowing in mud, or standing in water to escape summer flies, herding in season, called "Wapiti" by the Iroquois Indians, and miscalled elk by whites, the animal is glorified in scores of geographical names upon the American map. He was exterminated by sportsmen and gunners in Pennsylvania about 1850.

91

Moose. 132. (*Alces americanus.*) Gigantic, reddish brown, heavy-lipped, small-eyed, armed with very broad palmate antlers, with long fore and short hind legs, and neck not adapted to grazing, the immense deerlike moose, known to the white man in the northern pine forests of Maine and Canada, feeds upon the leaves, buds, and

bark, of trees or hillside bushes, or wades in the mud for the roots of the yellow pond lily. Hunters lure it to death with birch bark trumpets imitating the cow moose's call. Though probably absent in Pennsylvania in the colonial period, its bones found in Durham Cave, Bucks county, show that it ranged the Delaware Valley in earlier Indian times. Similar north European species nearly extinct.

132

Forging a Chain. 118. The white-hot links of iron are welded around each other by hammer blows against the adjacent segments, fluxed with borax at the right moment.

118

Spinning Wool. 116. By means of a short wooden rod, knobbed at the end, the woman sets the large wool wheel whirring, and this by a woolen strap, whirls the spindle, which winds on the thread as she measures it between thumb and forefinger of her left hand

116

grasping the carded roll of raw wool. Disused about 1830. Rare instances of use 1860-'80.

Oil Well. 117. When the narrow bored petroleum pump hole, having become clogged at a great depth, is blasted, by dropping a pointed iron weight (go-devil) upon a dynamite cartridge, the oil pressed upward by subterranean gas, bursts skyward in vapor above the derrick. Petroleum, used by Indians as a medical lubricant, or burned for sport when floating as an iridescent scum on Oil Creek, was applied about 1850 in western Pennsylvania as a world illuminant, revolutionizing all ancient lighting appliances. It had burned spontaneously at Baku on the Caspian Sea since prehistoric time, as an in-

117

spiration to the earliest Parsee fire worshippers.

Seal of Germantown. 122. A three-petaled clover leaf is surrounded with the Latin inscription S I G-I L L U M G E R-M A N O P O L I-TANUM, translated, Seal of the German Commonwealth.

122

The Loon. 121. (*Urinator imber.*) The remarkable bird walks with difficulty, rises to fly at a long angle with great effort, but dives like the otter to outstrip and catch the darting fish. When migrating to or from its northern nest, the loon halts to rest upon inland water, the farmer rushes for his gun.

121

Coal Miner. 131. Member of a threatening army rebellious against ancient economic conditions, the modern coal miner, lamp in hat, crouches in the propped subterranean gallery, pumped free of water or fire damp, to dig with a pick axe, lumps of hard or soft (anthracite or bituminous) coal, from the deep strata of the Susquehanna, Lehigh or Allegheny mines.

Coal Dealer's Wagon. 129. With a loud hissing noise, a load of anthracite coal is shot from the coal wagon's body, elevated upon cog-wheels, down a long sheet iron trough,

131

129

(**129** Continued)

through a wall or pavement hole, into the cellar coal bin.

Wild Duck. 130. Everywhere p u r s u e d by sportsmen, represented by many species, whether nesting in Pennsylvania or the far north, migrating at railroad speed high in air, in Y-shaped flocks, lured by wooden decoys, stalked from blinds, retrieved when dying in the water by so-called

Chesapeake Bay dogs (bred from a Labrador original in 1807), courting death or danger, whenever in season he lights for food or rest on pond river or bay, the wild duck outclasses in the typical form of the celery fed canvasback, all lauded products of the American kitchen.

Liberty Bell. 127. A greatly valued national relic kept at the State House in Philadelphia. In size 12 by 4 feet, weighing 2080 pounds, with motto from Leviticus "Proclaim Liberty," and stamped with order of assembly, caster's

130

name, advertisement and date 1753. It rang at several crises in the Revolutionary War with England, tolled at national funerals, and was displayed at national exhibitions. It cracked tolling for Chie Justice Marshall, July 8th, 1835.

127

Grapes. 126. The European grape having produced wine for eighteen centuries, when transplanted to the garden of the Pennsylvanian farmer and generally neglected, though remaining sweet and edible, so as to outrival the native fox and chicken grape, or flavor a home-brewed, sugared, acid beverage miscalled wine, whether

deteriorated by soil, climate, or lack of skill, in spite of extensive efforts in California, New Jersey, New York, etc., no longer (1908) produces for the American the ancient drink of his European ancestors.

Skunk. 125. (*Mephilis putida.*) With long fur richly painted in black, white or brown, hiding by day in wood pile or ruined cellar, the nocturnal, chicken-killing skunk, celebrated and dreaded because of the pungent overpowering defensive liquor cast by it

126

125

(**125** Continued)
at its enemies, defies the farmer's efforts at its extermination.

Keystone. 119¼. Pennsylvania coming to be called the Keystone State from its geographical position upon the map, by newspapers in the nineteenth century, the pattern of a keystone was used as an emblem of the state.

119¼

Chicken. 390. Probably descended from the wild chicken (*Gallus ferrugineus*) of India, and domesticated by man in prehistoric times, ever-present follower of humanity, and contributor to its progress with flesh, feathers and eggs, the domestic chicken, unknown in precolumbian America, has been more indispensable to man than the food-producing pig, if less so than the labor-contributing horse, the milk and leather-producing cow, and the wool-furnishing sheep.

390

Fox. 399. (*Vulpes fulvus.*) Sly, stealthy, slit-eyed, night-hunting, cleanly, devourer of birds chickens mice moles squirrels fish beetles or fruit, less swift than his European cousin, whether as the red fox of the north, or as the grey fox of the south, the celebrated animal, either burrowing in the earth, or living in rocks or hollow trees, is respected and hated by man. Driven into nets or dug out for extermination, until about 1650 in Britain, the fox began to allure the red-coated hunter and his hounds by the end of the 17th century. Thenceforward, protected as a target for sport, glorified by his destroyer in the fun of pictures, horns, hounds, redcoats, Irish reels, club rooms and balls, he becomes the type of the national sport of England transferred to America.

399

Battleship. 373. Heavy plates of steel rivetted together form the sides, water-tight compartments, gun rooms, turrets and decks, of the modern wood-fitted battleship, upon which the modern sailor, no longer concerned with tar ropes masts and sails, is drilled as a

373

385

mechanic and gunner. The mosaic shows a battleship at anchor near a city wharf.

The Butterfly. 385. Through one of the most marvelous changes in nature, sometimes lasting over winter, by way of egg laid upon a twig, voracious, l e a f - e a t i n g, skin-molting caterpillar, pseudo-death as a grub mummy wrapped in self-made coffin, long sleep and resurrection, the butterfly, cancelling in winged beauty the caterpillar's harm, emerges upon the lap of summer to out-vie the fairest of her flowers.

The Muskrat. 370. (*Fiber zibethicus.*) The amphibious prolific muskrat, inhabiting lakes and streams, invading cultivated lands, threatening dams and canals, destroying the water lily and lotus where they had flourished before, defies man's efforts to dig him out and exterminate him, and increases rather than disappears before the same civilization which, in exterminating the blood-letting mink which had filled the water rats' galleries with blood in the past, has withdrawn from the life struggle the muskrat's worst enemy.

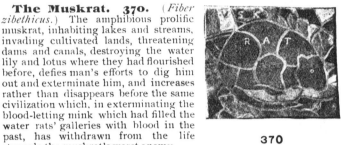

370

315

Casting Iron. 315. Blow a stream of air into a confined fire of coke or charcoal, piled upon lumps of iron ore mixed with pieces of lime stone. When the molten metal, beneath masses of floating slag, runs out a clay tap hole, ladle it into moulds made of stiff, fine-grained, ferrugineous (casting) sand, or let it run free by way of a long trough-shaped open sand furrow (the sow), into smaller side troughs (the pigs). Able to soften iron by heat and shape the soft spongy mass with a hammer, since the dawn of history or at the end of the Bronze Age, man, though long previously familiar with bronze casting, has only been able thus to melt the stubborn iron ore and cast it in moulds, since the 15th century.

Weasel. 401. (*Putor-ius noveboracensis.*) Sometimes turning all white in winter, brown-backed, keen-scented, night-hunting, wholesale destroyer and blood sucker of rats, mice, moles, frogs, birds and chickens.

The Telegraph. 342. By means of "creepers," namely steel prongs strapped to his feet and legs,

401

the workman, armed with a wire cutter, has ascended the smooth pole to splice a storm broken wire, and repair the mechanism of one of the greatest inventions of modern times. (Many original inven-

(**342** Continued)
tors 1747-1837. Many improving
inventors 1837-1890. Systematized
by Morse after 1837).

Blue Jay. 381. (*Cyanocitta
cristata.*) Beautiful t y r a n n i c a l
alarmist, omnivorous flesh and
vegetable eater, egg-sucking, nest-
ling eating, oppressor of other
birds, and appropriator of half-
built nests, the blue jay, hunting
apples, pears, beechnuts, acorns,
insects, cocoons, barberries, blackberries, etc., with startling **cries**
flashes quick gleams of ultramarine
through the gray woods of autumn
or the green
l e a v e s of
summer.

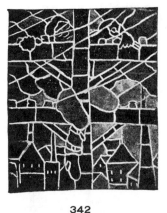

342

The Grasshopper. 95. Sweet as
the song of the meadow lark or scent of new
mown hay, charming the recollection of
thousands of human minds aged in the toil
of cities, rises the universal memory of an
infant form, hatless and barefoot, chasing

381

the ever present grasshopper, who with immense
fascinating leaps, wins the
race on the soft grass or
prickly stubble fields of
summer. The "grasshop-
per war," an exterminating
battle of an old Delaware
and Susquehanna Valley
myth, came, according to
the farmer's wife's tale,
from the overleaping by a
grasshopper of a s i n e w
boundary s t r e t c h e d between two Indian camps.

95

The chasing children of
the rival tribes quarrel, and the squaws take their part; the braves
intervene, and then a desperate resulting battle strews the
river shores, as at Durham, or fills the mound, as at Connewago,
with skulls.

Oysters. 105. (*Ostrea virginiana.*) Ancient seaside heaps,
"kitchen middens," of oyster and other shells, from Maine to
Florida, and Alaska to California, prove
that the Indians roasted and ate oysters
for many centuries. Stewed, panned,
roasted, raw, deviled, broiled, fried,
steamed, boxed, or brazed, the American
oyster, less highly flavored than its
European cousin, raked from marine
estuaries to be rapidly distributed by
railroads, soon became the familiar staple
of the city restaurant and barroom cook,
and as stewed with milk, a national dish.
Oysters were gluttonously eaten raw on
wagers in the fifties, at country eating
houses and old fashioned oyster suppers.

105

Inland lanes and roads paved with their shells (1908) prove an immense increase in their consumption.

215

Heckewaelder Preaching.
215. The Moravian missionary, minister of Christ's peace and brotherhood among Indians, venerable, noble, beloved, upholding a friendship for the red man, equal to and long outliving that proclaimed by Penn, here preaches to the Lenape after a common fashion, standing upon a stump in the partly cleared woods.

Flax Reel. 168.
From a standard set upon a tripod, four pegged arms turned horizontally to wind off flax thread into skeins from the spindle. Sometimes set upon a forked sapling and easily made at home without turning lathe. Disused with the spinning wheel about 1835.

Skunk. 85.
(*Mephitis putida.*) With long fur richly painted in black white or brown, hiding by day in the wood pile or ruined cellar, the nocturnal chicken-killing skunk, celebrated and dreaded because of the pungent overpowing defensive liquor cast by it at its enemies, defies the farmer's efforts at its extermination.

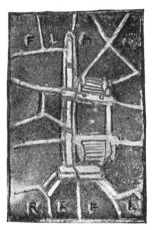

108

85

The Grasshopper. 82.
Sweet as the song of the meadow lark or scent of new mown hay, charming the recollection of thousands of human minds aged in the toil of cities, rises the universal memory of an infant form, hatless and barefoot, chasing the ever present grasshopper, who with immense fascinating leaps, wins the race on the soft grass or prickly stubble fields of summer. The "grasshopper war," an e x t e r m i n a t i n g battle of an old Delaware and Susquehanna m y t h, came according to the farmer's wife's tale, from the overleaping by a grasshopper of a sinew boundary stretched between two Indian camps. The chasing children

82

of the rival tribes quarrel, and the squaws take their part. The braves intervene, and then a desperate resulting battle strews the river shores, as at Durham, or fills the mound, as at Connewago, with skulls.

Oysters. 111.
(*Ostrea virginiana.*) Ancient seaside heaps "kitchen middens," of oyster and other shells, from Maine to Florida, and from Alaska to California, prove that Indians roasted and ate oysters for many centuries. Stewed, panned, roasted, raw, deviled, broiled, fried, steamed, boxed or brazed, the American oyster, less

(**III** Continued)

highly flavored than its European cousin, raked from marine estuaries to be rapidly distributed by railroads, soon became the familiar staple of the city restaurant and barroom cook, and as stewed with milk, a national dish. Oysters were gluttonously eaten raw on wagers in the fifties at country eating houses and old fashioned oyster suppers. Inland lanes and roads paved with their shells (1908) prove an immense increase in their consumption.

111

Dutch Oven. 112. A cast iron lidded pot, usual diameter about 20 inches. Height about 9. Place in it the risen dough for bread, then set on the convex lid and bury the pot in the hot embers of the open fire. Lift on or off the coals by the hinged wrought iron handle, whose hooks slip in or out of the clasp holes against the rim. Discontinued with open fire cooking about 1830-40. Still used by western camping parties, though but a meagre substitute for the bake oven of brick or clay. A rather uncommon farmyard relic in 1897. Handles and lids generally lost or the latter used as watering troughs for chickens.

112

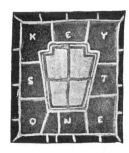

139

Keystone. 139. Pennsylvania coming to be called the Keystone State from its geographical position upon the map, by newspapers in the nineteenth century, the pattern of a keystone was since used as an emblem of the state.

Pioneer Rifleman. 359. A marksman of deadly aim from continual shooting at Indians and animals, the Pennsylvanian pioneer, armed at first with a transatlantic gun, barreled with a spiral bore to make the flying leaden bullet rotate, (rifle of Edward Marshall the Indian walker, made 1737-'50 at Rothenburg Germany), began making his own "Lancaster" and "Kentucky" rifles at Reading, Lancaster and elsewhere by the end of the 18th century. Though subject to speedy annihilation in a bayonet charge, and denied a place in European armies by Napoleon, organized bands of these deadly slow firing Indian fighters, with coon skin caps buckskin shirts and fringed leggings did great service in frontier battles, and at New Orleans in 1815, where the riflemen, lying behind cotton bales and supplied by boys with continually reloaded extra rifles, destroyed at a distance the British army, killed its general, and won the battle in a few minutes.

359

Squirrel. 140. (*Sciurus carolinensis.*) Having survived the enmity of the farmer, who shoots and eats the squirrel or imprisons him in a tin cage and treadmill, the animal finds peace in

140

(**140** Continued)
the city park and town grove, where children tame and feed him.

Flying Squirrel. 114. (*Sciuropterus volans.*) Nocturnal, dwelling in large gnawed holes in dead trees old house cornices deserted garrets or summer houses, sometimes imprisoned in tin cages by the farmer's boy, the beautiful flying squirrel outvies in celebrity many larger animals, by flitting at night diagonally from tree to tree upon winglike extensions of its leg skin.

Wooden Plough. 101. Homemade plough, ironed by country blacksmith, and set with a wooden mould board, probably universal in the Atlantic States before 1800. Sometimes protected with sheet iron or as on the eastern shore of Maryland, with bull-fish skin nailed to the

114

mould board to save wear. Often rehandled with a cow's horn. Generally superseded by iron mould boards about 1810.

Letitia House. 137. Small brick house with white painted wood facings, built by William Penn in 1683, in a garden between Front, Second and Market streets, and Black Horse Alley, Philadelphia.

101

Penn's residence for about one year; capitol of the Province until about 1700; given to his daughter Letitia who sold it to William Eastman. Twice serving as an inn (Rising Sun and Wool Sack), and afterward neglected and nearly destroyed by modern city growth. In 1882 removed and re-erected at its present (1908) site in Fairmount Park.

Black Bear. 115. (*Ursus americanus.*) With dog and gun, man finds a bloody amusement in rapidly exterminating the honey loving, ant fish and root eating, vegetarian and carnivorous black bear. Glossy black, brown-cheeked, dog-fearing,

137

harmless (unless when with cubs or in self defense), the tree-climbing hibernating animal, was reverenced, almost worshipped, yet hunted and eaten by Indians in the primeval forest. Close kin to the brown bear of Europe, the once abundant black bear in vain

115

(**115** Continued)
retires to inaccessible places, to escape the relentless and untiring hatred of his human pursuer.

Churning Butter. 136.

The woman works a vertical wooden piston, set upon cruciform splashing arms, and projecting through a lid hole in the barrel-shaped churn half-filled with cream. Used in Eastern Pennsylvania until about 1850. Still in use

near Peekskill on the Hudson, and there (1907) sometimes attached to a (now factory-made, previously home-constructed) treadmill, worked by a dog (the dog-churn).

Red-Headed Woodpecker. 138.

(*Melanerpes erythrocephalus.*) You must search among the painted birds of the tropics for a rival to this magnificent insect hunter, who startles the silent woods with sudden resonant drumming upon dead tree limbs, or, darting in red black and white through summer leafage, protests in his thrilling life, against the farmer who would shoot him because he eats cherries, the un-

136

taught boy who destroys him for fun, or the woman who wears his distorted skin or wings upon her hat.

Skunk. 142.

(*Mephitis putida.*) With long fur richly painted in black white or brown, hiding by day in the wood pile or ruined cellar, the nocturnal chicken-killing

138

skunk, celebrated and dreaded because of the pungent overpowering defensive liquor cast by it at its enemies, defies the farmer's efforts at its extermination.

The Locomotive Engine. 107.

For ten centuries preceding the date 1820, no such revolutionary change in the habits of man through his equipment with labor-saving devices, has occurred, as between 1820 and the present time. More potently than electricity,

142

107

(**107** Continued)

gunpowder, printing, coal, iron or petroleum, the locomotive engine has probably worked · to produce this result. With its new rapid transfer of men and merchandise, customs a thousand years old, tools, utensils, implements, things home and hand made, vanished as if by magic. Largest type of locomotive of Philadelphia make (1902), heavier, stronger, and of broader wheel guage, than its European rival.

The Dog. 148. (*Canis familiaris.*) When first domesticated by the North American Indian, or prehistoric old world savage, the wolf or jackal lost its ferocity to become the affectionate dog, an epoch was marked in the history of man. And the thinker may associate with the dog another epoch in man's higher e v o l u t i o n, when as now (1909) the human conscience strangely awakes, to enter upon a memorable struggle. Many unselfish champions of mercy and love, rejecting the alleged cure of their own diseases, arm themselves for a world wide conflict with thousands of modern doctors

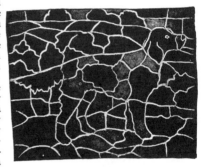

148

and students, who proclaiming advantage to the human race, cut open (with or without pain deadening drugs), disembowel, inocculate with disease, (vivisect) the living dog to help their surgery or medicine, or illustrate facts (previously known or unknown) to their scholars. Friendly, fleet, intelligent, trained to a multitude of uses besides hunting birds and animals, carnivorous, clinging to filthy habits and food, often unselfish, faithful, devoted beyond compare, the dog has followed close upon the human wanderer from the darkness of prehistoric time. What more remarkable moment than when the highest human education, the loftiest Christianity, forgets its pride, and humbles its desires, to find inspiration in the friendship of a dog.

144

Opossum. 144. (*Didelphys virginiana.*) Sluggish, sleepy, helpless, death feigning, fruit insect and chicken eating, hunted of old and eaten with delight by the American slave and free, continually caught and killed by the farmer, the celebrated prolific American marsupial, ghastly in hair and skin, unknown in Europe, and related to the Australian kangaroo, continuing to rear about 36 young per year in three litters in its extraordinary breast pouch, survives its human enemy, and still harbors unsuspected close to the farmer's henroost and haystack, or in his hollow apple tree.

Man Using Frow. 147. With an L-shaped knife blade held upon a cylindrical section of white oak trunk set on a chopping block, the man splits with the grain, thin sections off the piece, by blows of a short large-headed wooden club. These shingles thus split, and afterwards pared where necessary with a draw knife, roofed early houses and log cabins. Homemade shingles split and used at Wormansville, Bucks county, 1896.

147

Grapes. 149. The European grape having produced wine for eighteen centuries, transplanted to the garden of the Pennsylvanian farmer, has been generally neglected. Though remaining sweet and edible, so as to outrival the native fox and chicken grape, or flavor a sugared acid home made wine, it has deteriorated, whether by soil, climate or lack of skill; and in spite of extensive efforts in California, New Jersey and New York, etc., no longer (1908) produces for the American the ancient drink of his European ancestors.

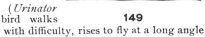

149

The Loon. 150. (*Urinator imber.*) The remarkable bird walks with difficulty, rises to fly at a long angle with great effort, but dives like the otter to outstrip and catch the darting fish. When the loon migrating to or from its northern nest, halts to rest upon inland water, the farmer rushes for his gun.

150

Woman Baking. 145. The brick fire chamber in a stone oven built against into or outside the house, and often opening into the kitchen fireplace, is heated with a wood fire. When the hot embers are raked out, and the oven cleaned with a damp swab, the bread loaves are pushed in or pulled out upon a long-handled shovel of wood or iron (the peel). Apple peach pumpkin huckleberry mince squash and and other forms of the familiar American pie, were developed from English original types, in these ovens.

Snapping Turtle. 133. (*Chelydra serpentina.*) Ferocious, carnivorous, devourer of frogs tadpoles and young ducks, only half-protected by his under shell, always fighting in self-defense, most active of the turtle tribe in Pennsylvania, inhabiting the muddy bottom of mill ponds, the snapping turtle, grand trophy of the torch light fisherman and wandering boy, sometimes caught with red flannel

145

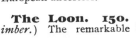

133

(**133** Continued)
on a fish hook, is the origin of a renowned "snapper soup" popular in country restaurants.

Conestoga Wagon. 134. The immense ponderous schooner-shaped wagon of probable German d e s c e n t, named from the site of its earliest make along the Conestoga Creek in Lancaster county, with homespun linen cover stretched on wooden bows, and drawn by four to

six walking horses, often equipped with bells, transported freight south of New England lines of sea and lake transport and across the Alleghenies, before railroads were built. In lighter form, a wagon of national type, celebrated as the "prairie schooner," it bore the American emigrant and his family "Westward Ho."

Reaping With the Sickle. 143. Lean forward and seizing a large bunch of wheat or rye with the left hand,

134

143

cut the stalks near the ground by drawing the keen serrated narrow sickle blade across them from left to right. Then, as the mosaic shows, you reap as your ancestors did from Egyptian times until about 1820, when, at the advent of the old European grain cradle, and Hainault scythe (dispensing with stalk grasping), and finally the reaping machine, the greatest craft of husbandry changed suddenly and forever.

Bat. 135. (*Vespertilio.*) Marvelous, weird, night-seeing, alert after a day trance, hanging head downward on wing claws, in caves hollow trees open cellars or ruined barns, sometimes, for mother love, weighted on the wing with clinging brood, the fantastic bats enter the open window of the lamp lit bedroom, snuff the k i t c h e n candle, chase twilight beetles

135

over tree top and lawn, or as demons of the night breeze, tease the boy players of "kick-the-wicket," who followed them of old shouting as in the Maryland child's rhyme—

"Leather winged bat, fly under my hat
And I'll give you a ham of bacon."

Kittens. 384. Transplanted from Europe as an inheritance from savage human ancestors who had domesticated it probably before

(**384** Continued)

384

Egyptian times, everywhere familiar as a household pet, kept by man as a destroyer of rats and mice long before the Norway rat invaded England in the 16th century, or followed European discoverers to America, the cat vies with the dog in human popularity.

Reconciliation of North and South. 379. The mosaic represents

the reconciliation of two survivors of the Civil War, once soldier enemies, now farmers, meeting after thirty years to shake hands on their old battlefield at Gettysburg, upon the noted reunion of surviving veterans in 1903.

Gettysburg. 378. A struggle between citizens of the United States at

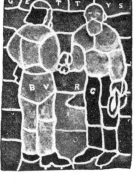

379

378

Gettysburg in 1863, decided against the continued inconsistent existence of negro slavery in the liberty asserting United States, and against the division of the Republic into two nations.

Stephen Collins Foster. 382. The mosaic shows the first musical bar of the song called "Old Folks at Home" often known as "The "Suwannee River," inscribed on the roof of a riverside log cabin. The background is stamped with the initials S. C. F. standing for Stephen Collins Foster, most original song writer of the United States, born at Pittsburg in 1826, and principal originator of Anglo-African music. Author of "Old

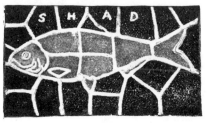

382

Kentucky Home," "Old Uncle Ned," "Carry Me Back to Old Virginny," "Hard Times," "Nelly Bly," "Old Dog Tray," etc. The music of Foster, better remembered than his name, outvies in inspiration to Americans, the reputation of many founders warriors and statesmen.

Shad. 373. (*Clupea sapidissima.*) Netted while

373

ascending in shoals eastern seaboard rivers in the spring to spawn, protected by law, lost in winter in the ocean's depth, the immensely prolific sensitive graceful shad, dying in captivity, or at the friction

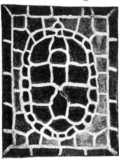

of nets, was fried in the long handled frying pan, broiled on the gridiron by the open fire of the old farm kitchen, or roasted on a plank by the bonfire of the Delaware River fisherman.

Indian Rock Picture. 341.

Symbolizing the mystic forces of nature in a conglomerate shape of bird reptile and demon, as in the wild worship of many primitive peoples, this wierd outline, pecked with the points of hard sharp stones, two centuries ago at least, by Indians, comprises one of a group of freshet-worn figures, on the east face of Big Indian Rock in the Susquehanna rapids at Safe Harbor.

341

Drawing Water at the Well Sweep. 380.

By means of a balanced bucket bearing pole, weighted at the base and hinged upon a post, the woman, leaning against the wooden well curb, lowers the empty bucket, fastened upon a long stick, and lifts it again full from the well. Ancient apparatus in general use until 1840. Surviving (1909) in wilder mountain regions. Still common in 1907 near Cambridge, Maryland.

380

Turtle Carapace. 348.

Celebrated in white man's history and legend, venerated as an emblem of wisdom by the Indian, the sluggish unwieldy turtle, heavily armored above and below by carapace and plastron, resists without much effort the attack of many enemies; sometimes defying the tearing of eagle's beak and talons, as when, if the legend be true, a bird of prey high in air, killed the Greek poet, Aeschylus by dropping a tortoise upon his head.

348

Death of General Braddock. 400.

General Braddock fell at the defeat of his Colonial troops when openly charging ambushed French and Iroquois Indians, who shot their rifles from behind trees, at the battle of Great Meadows in 1756.

Shoeing the Horse. 391.

All horses in the new world, the wild prairie or pampas breeds Indian pony and Mexican mustang included, are of imported transatlantic stock, domesticated by old world savages in the stone age. The once abundant American horse, having perished in an unex-

400

(**391** Continued)

plained sudden manner, as his fossil bones show, in post-glacial times, was replaced by the European animal, chief historic transporter of man and merchandise, contributor of untold unthanked labor for many milleniums before steam, and of inestimable help in human progress. Free-hoofed for soft ground by nature, but shod with iron shoes for stony soil since the dawn of civilization.

391

Oil Well. 386. When the narrow bored pump hole, having become clogged at a great depth, is blasted by dropping a pointed iron weight (go-devil) upon a dynamite cartridge, the oil pressed upward by subterranean gas, bursts skyward in vapor above the derrick. Petroleum was used by Indians as a medical lubricant, or burned for sport as an iridescent scum on Oil Creek, before its application in Western Pennsylvania as a world illuminant revolutionized all ancient lighting appliances. It had burned spontaneously at Baku on the Caspian Sea since prehistoric time, giving inspiration to the earliest Parsee fire-worshippers.

386

Rattlesnake. 374. (*Crotalus horridus.*) Less poisonous than the cobra of India, or the fer de lance of Martinique, devourer of small rodents, the deadly rattlesnake, where he survives in the Appalachians from New Hampshire to Florida, is justly dreaded by man. About four feet long, sluggish, coiling, rattling, reluctantly striking, the brown or blackish yellow diaper-striped snake was avoided and venerated by Indians and white men, and but very rarely conciliated by snake loving mountaineers, who dare to pick up the fanged reptile in their hands.

374

Sheep. 394. Unknown in America before Columbus, domesticated by man in Europe at an unknown period in prehistoric time, the gentle timorous grass-eating wool-bearing sheep, as the principal origin of woven clothes, has been of inestimable importance to man since the dawn of history. Spanish (merino), and English breeds (Cotswold, Liecestershire, Southdown, etc.), were brought to the United States in the 16th century and later. Variously mixed on the farm, and source of supply for housewife's wool wheel, the country loom, and farmer's homespun linsey-woolsey clothes, after the clearing of the forest.

Boy Rolling Hoop. 393. Alternating his sport with games of marbles, the village rather than country boy, chases his rolling hoop (an

394

393

(**393** Continued)
iron or wooden barrel hoop, beaten with a stick) in 1908, as he chased it in France in 1348 (according to an illuminated missal in the Bodlean Library of old Oxford). The ancient sport common (1908) in Britain, north and south Germany, Scandinavia, Italy and France.

Typewriter. 388. Human handwriting with a pen rapidly dis-

388

appears from the transactions of commerce after 1880 to be supplanted by the printed manuscript of the typewriter, developed from the inventions of Wheatstone and Foucault about 1855. Inked type dart against the surface of a revolving sheet of paper rapidly forming words, while the writer, as shown in the mosaic, plays with both hands upon the keyboard of the instrument.

Iron Miner. 376. Iron the master metal, marking when utilized by man after bronze, an epoch in human history, is here as an ore dug with a crow bar by the miner, from its native vein as sometimes exposed upon the open hillside.

Cricket. 387. The familiar black insect, proclaiming the wane of summer by the tinkling of his rubbed **wings**

376

about mid-August, belongs to a numerous family, greatly beloved in the form of its celebrated representative the house cricket (*Grillus domesticus*), who finding nooks of winter shelter indoors, sings undismayed near the open hearth of the old kitchen.

387

Redbud. 392. (*Cercis canadensis.*) Where the southern redbud or Judas tree grows wild in the Susquehanna woods stand beneath the yet leafless

392

boughs gleaming in crimson blossoms, and while the bees hum and the spring zephyr brings memories of southern forests, forget even the snowy shad bush, and the white vernal glory of the matchless dogwood.

Rabbit. 396. (*Lepus floridanus.*) With brown cinnamon and gray fur, and

396

(**396** Continued)

white under tail, very prolific, subsisting on roots and vegetables, burrowing, crouching till almost touched, very fleet, doubling to escape dogs, the rabbit defies extermination in spite of gunners in season, minks weasels crows and hawks. Hard is the heart which unmoved to pity, sees the terrified rabbit crouching in clear view by log or weed stalk, while the dogs bark and race in distant circles.

wheat sheaf (agriculture), plow (agriculture), wreathed with Indian corn (agriculture), and lacking quarterings for iron or petroleum. The whole ill designed in realistic spirit, a misconceived picture, rather than a conventionalized pattern.

Turtle Carapace. 397.

Celebrated in white man's history and legend, venerated as an emblem of wisdom by the Indian, the sluggish unwieldy reptile, heavily armored above and below by carapace and plastron, resists without much effort the attack of many enemies; some-

The Arms of Pennsylvania.

375. Two rampant horses support a shield emblazoned with ship (commerce),

375

times defying the tearing of eagle's beak and talons, as when, if the legend be true, a bird of prey high in air, killed the Greek poet Aeschylus by dropping a tortoise upon his head.

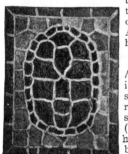

397

Soft Shelled Crab. 398. (*Callinectes hastatus.*) The maritime blue crab

in its shell (hard shell), or having recently cast its shell in summer (soft shell), inhabits the muddy beaches of the Delaware Chesapeake and Atlantic tide water coasts. Deviled broiled fried hashed, dressed in many ways, it ranks like the terrapin oyster and canvasback duck as a boasted national dish.

398

Baltimore Oriole. 383. (*Icterus galbula.*) Gleaming black and orange through the summer boughs of hickory apple oak and maple, named after the Irish town Baltimore indirectly through the heraldic colors of Lord Baltimore founder of Maryland, destroyer of insects, brilliant musician, migrating in winter to Mexico, the magnificent "hanging bird," in nest building gladly seizes upon the strings rags and lint of the modern white American, minus which in the shadows

383

of the great forest, the oriole must have built his hanging pouchlike nest with greater trouble of vegetable fibre and twigs.

The Iron Miner. 377. Mighty medium of modern progress, iron the master metal, marking when utilized by man after bronze, an epoch in human history, is here dug by the miner with a pickaxe from its native vein.

Wild Cat. 152. (*Lynx rufus.*) Yellowish brown, short-tailed, with hair tufts on ears spotted with dark brown or black, scaring its prey with a wild scream, sleeping in hollow trees caves and rock shelters,

377

destroying young birds in the nest, mincing catnip, wallowing in strong scented herbs, stalking rabbits and grouse in the twilight of dawn or eve, unearthing mice or watching at squirrel holes, the wild cat springs from ambush or overhead bough upon his larger prey. This relative of the domestic cat lion tiger leopard and fossil American sabre-toothed smilo-

152

don, has been driven by his old enemy the Pennsylvanian farmer to the few remaining forest fastnesses of the Alleghenies.

Snapping Turtle. 172. (*Chelydra serpentina.*) Ferocious, carnivorous, devourer of frogs tadpoles and young ducks, only half protected by his under shell, always fighting in self-defense, the snapping turtle, most active of the turtle tribe in Pennsylvania, inhabits the

172

muddy bottom of the mill-pond. Grand trophy of torch light fisherman and wandering boy, sometimes caught with red flannel on a fish hook, the fierce reptile is the origin of a renowned "snapper soup" popular in country restaurants.

Loon. 157. (*Urinator imber.*) The remarkable bird walks with difficulty, rises to fly at a long angle with great effort, but dives like the otter to outstrip and catch the darting fish. When migrating to or from its northern nest the loon halts to rest upon inland water, the farmer rushes for his gun.

157

Keystone. 158. Pennsylvania coming to be called the Keystone State from its geographical position upon the map by

(158 Continued)

158

newspapers in the nineteenth century, the pattern of a keystone was since used as an emblem of the state.

House Pump. 153. A stout log of sky-blue white oak, hand bored by means of a graduated series of long handled pod augers, plugged with a spout, and adjusted with a wrought iron handle. Having superseded at the farm well, the balanced pole, the ancient windlass, balanced buckets, and hooked staff, the homemade pump was generally replaced about 1870-'90 by the light factory-made gaudily painted hand pump of similar mechanism. Where the old pump stands by the barn yard wall, the innocent boy, coaxed of a frosty morning to hunt *elbedritches* (the furred goblin animal of the Pennsylvania German myth), is fastened by the tip of his steaming tongue to the frosty iron, which he has been induced to lick.

Chickens. 161. Descended from the wild chicken (*Gallus ferrugineus*) of India, and domesticated by Asiatic savages in unknown prehistoric time, the chicken, having long contributed to humanity's progress with eggs flesh

153

and feathers, has been artificially hatched by Arabs in Egypt since the middle ages, from eggs placed in earthen ovens, and daily turned. (the origin of the modern incubator).

House Fly. 175. (*Musca domestica*). The familiar, buzzing, warmth-loving, house-infesting, disease spreading insect, grown in filth garbage and horse manure, within a month, through egg, maggot, and fly, was probably introduced from Europe with the horse, by first settlers.

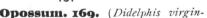

161

Opossum. 169. (*Didelphis virginiana.*) Sluggish, sleepy, helpless, death-feigning, fruit insect and chicken eating, hunted of old and eaten with delight by the southern American, slave and free. Often caught and killed by the northern farmer, the celebrated prolific American marsupial, ghastly in hair and skin, unknown in Europe, is related to the Australian kangaroo. It continues to rear about 36 young per year in three

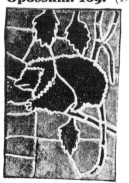

169

175

litters, in its extraordinary breast pouch, survives its human enemy, and still harbors unsuspected close to the farmer's henroost and haystack, or in his hollow apple tree.

163

Shelling Corn. 163. The man throws the husked ears of maize into a hopper set against a log bristling with short iron spikes. This revolving as he turns a crank, tears off the grain and casts away the cob. Homemade about 1800.

Oysters. 156. (*Ostrea virginiana.*) Ancient seaside heaps "kitchen middens," of oyster and other shells, from Maine to Florida, and from Alaska to California, prove that Indians roasted and ate oysters for many centuries. Stewed, panned, roasted, deviled, broiled, fried, steamed, boxed, or brazed, the American oyster, less highly flavored than its European cousin, raked from marine estuaries to be rapidly distributed by railroads, soon became the familiar staple of the city restaurant and barroom cook, and, stewed with milk, a national dish. Oysters were gluttonously eaten raw on wagers in the fifties at country eating houses and old fashioned oyster suppers. Inland lanes and roads paved with their shells (1908) prove an immense increase in their consumption.

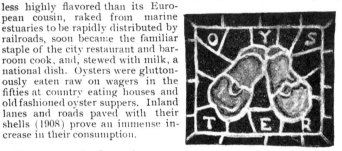

156

German School. 155. When the English language became

155

compulsory in Pennsylvanian public schools in 1854, several old customs disappeared in the German speaking districts, such as the teaching of music by ancient notation inscribed in chalk upon the ceiling beams, instruction in illuminated writing (Fractur); or the punishment of children with the box brille, or leather horned (goats) spectacles. Yet the children taught in English, still (in 1908) play at recess in German.

Chicken Cock. 154. Domesticated by Eastern Asiatics from the jungle fowl (*Gallus ferrugineus*) more than a millenium

B. C., graceful, many colored, red-combed, courageous, the barnyard cock, everywhere familiar companion of man in his migrations, head of a race vitalizing humanity with eggs flesh and feathers, herald of dark and dawn, has been patterned in Christendom as a vane to mark the wind's change since its crow marked Peter's denial, hence in shape or name (German hahn, English cock) applied to the turning lids of ancient lamps, and modern valves or spigots. Since Homer's time, the bird has been as deeply interwoven with man's life literature and history as the horse or cow.

154

Cherries. 174. (*Prunus cerasus.*) Rival of the strawberry, beloved of boys and birds, associated with the flavor of cherry bounce and pie, the delicious European fruit, in its best known forms of oxheart, pie cherry, or black cherry, when freshly imported, and grown by the log cabin of the pioneer, may have been seen by the Indian before his expulsion from Pennsylvania. The Pennsylvanian must thank the horticulture of his European ancestors for this fair fruit of early summer, brought to Europe by Lucullus the Roman epicure from Cerasus of Asiatic Pontus, to be cultivated for centuries in France England and Germany. If in Pennsyl-

174

vania degenerating in flavor, it has not failed in the magnificence of its white blossoms, which gladdening the road sides when the meadow lark sings his spring song, only yield in beauty to those which the Japanese wonder at on April seventh.

Type Setter. 164. The greater needs of knowledge justly destroyed a magnificent art, when printing, discovered about 1450, whether by Faust and Guttenburg, or by others, (though despised by the bibliophiles of the 16th century, such as Cardinal Bembo who would not have a printed book in his library), superseded book making by hand. Henceforth the art, revolutionizing all human knowledge, of assembling block letters into words and sentences, clamping them together to ink them and press them on paper, continued with little change until immensely facilitated in recent times through improvements upon many previous machines, by the invention (Lanston and Mergenthaler 1884), of casting the type from molten metal, while assembling them in immediate

164

response to a finger touch upon a key board like that of a typewriter.

Barrack. 160. A movable roof clasping four posts, pried up or let down upon iron pegs at the four corners, covers the hay stack. Common 1908 in Pennsylvania. Almost unknown in New England.

160

Moth. 162. (*Actias luna.*) Member of an immense prolific world-spread family, whether harmless to man or destructive of his food and clothes, transformed like the butterfly through marvelous changes of life death and resurection, the nocturnal moth, hidden by day, becomes a

162

household wonder of a summer night, as lured often to death by lamp glare through the open window, he flits ghost-like in velvet splendor to rest with wings spread flat upon the window sill or curtain.

Penn's Seal of Pennsylvania. 197.

197

Three ears of Indian corn dividing bunches of grapes, surrounded by the noble words TRUTH PEACE LOVE AND PLENTY, and encircled with flowers, symbolized the Christian ideals of George Fox and William Penn, which for a short time reflected a world-wide glory and promise upon the young commonwealth, and delighted the philosophers and philanthropists of the age.

Barn Owl. 141.

(*Strix pratincola.*) A very conspicuous yellow-brown owl staring blinking and bowing, when rarely seen in hollow tree deserted garret belfry or ruined barn hiding from the daylight. Destroyer

of field mice and moles, never of birds chickens and pigeons, hence a help to the agriculturalist, yet ruthlessly killed by man in boyish curiosity misguided sport woman's vanity or farmer's ignorance.

The Grasshopper. 176.

Sweet as the song of the meadow lark or scent of new mown hay, charming the recollection of thousands of human minds aged in the toil of cities, rises the universal memory of an infant form, hatless and barefoot, chasing

141

the ever present grasshopper, who with immense fascinating leaps wins the race on the soft grass or prickly stubble fields of summer. The "grasshopper war," an exterminating battle celebrated in an old Delaware and Susquehanna myth, came, according to the farmer's wife's tale, from the

176

over-leaping by a grasshopper of a sinew boundary stretched between two Indian camps. The chasing children of the rival tribes quarrel and the squaws take their part; the braves intervene, and then a desperate resulting battle strews the river shores, as at Durham, or fills the mound as at Connewago, with skulls.

The Pine. 167.

Sawed for boards hard or soft, yellow or white, or scored for exuding resin, origin of

167

pitch, the pine tree covers the northern hills and southern swamps. Notable in various forms, but most distinctive as the beautiful white pine (*Pinus strobus*), rivaling the cedar of Lebanon or the Deodar of India with its bare winglike limbs feathered only at the ends. Cut with the axe or movable saw, and floated down the stream in the form of trimmed logs, the white pine seems to approach extermination in Pennsylvania.

Cricket. 166. The familiar black insect family, proclaiming in late August the wane of summer, by the tinkling of rubbed wings, is greatly beloved in the form of its celebrated representative the house cricket (*Grillus domesticus*), who finding nooks of winter shelter indoors sang undismayed near the open hearth of the old kitchen.

166

Porcupine. 165. (*Erethizon dorsatus.*) Rolled into a ball of poisonous barbed bristles destructive to the tongue and mouth of wolf or wild cat, the porcupine defends itself against ferocious enemies, far exceeding it in strength. Tree climbing, greedy of salt, feeding upon the inner bark of elm, linden and hemlock trees, sometimes gnawing the bones of cave-buried animals for food, the non-hibernating animal who nests in a hollow tree, was hunted by Indians for open fire roasting and for its quills valued as decorations for belt pouch and moccasin.

165

Skillet. 168. A large thin cup of hammered iron with long handle, is set upon its three legs in the hot embers of the old open kitchen fire. Stew in it meat or vegetables or baby's pap in water or milk. Generally disused with open fire cooking about 1840.

Wild Duck. 171. Everywhere pursued by sportsmen, represented by many species whether nesting in Pennsylvania or the far north, migrating at railroad speed high in air in Y-shaped flocks, lured by wooden decoys, stalked

168

from blinds, retrieved when dying in the water by so called Chesapeake Bay dogs (bred from a Labrador original in 1807), courting death or danger whenever, in season, he lights for food or rest on pond river or bay, the wild duck out classes in the typical form of the celery fed canvasback, all lauded products of the American kitchen.

Blast Furnace. 178. An iron tower, pumping air and shooting flames, solves the problem long unsolved, of melting masses of iron ore mixed with coke and lime stone (smelting), or

171

remelting the product for casting. Until the middle ages, the smith, thus able from unknown antiquity to melt tin mixed with copper

178

(**178** Continued)

(bronze), and cast it in moulds, could only soften, not melt, the iron mass of more or less pure ore, and hammer (forge) it into shape.

The Oak. 170. (*Quercus.*) Long lived, colossal, durable, highly valued for wood bark and sawdust, represented by a multitude of varieties as the red, black, swamp, willow, chestnut, and pin oak, or as the familiar ashen-barked white oak, frequently marking the land boundaries in old deeds, the oak, though unknown in Australia and tropical Africa, ennobles the forests of Europe Asia and America in the north temperate zone.

170

Stagecoach. 183. The 18th century Americanized English stagecoach, of generally square low form in Pennsylvania, or egg-shaped with side doors boot and top seats, since about 1800 of New England make, generally painted yellow, and swung on leather straps, became celebrated in the sixties on the Deadwood, and other overland stage routes of California and the far west. Surviving (1900) in remote corners of New England.

183

inscription WILLIAM PENN PROPRIETOR AND GOVERNOR OF PENNSYLVANIA.

The Elm. 187. (*Ulmus americana.*) Less conspicuous and beloved for village shade than in New England, the white, American, or water elm of Pennsylvania, often vase-shaped in the outline of its plumed branches, loves water courses, and escapes the barbarism of Pennsylvania German village tree-topping, in moist woods. The most noted tree of its kind in Pennsylvania, venerated as shading the

Penn's Seal of Pennsylvania. 182. A shield with the arms of William Penn against a background adorned with scrolls and inscribed with the words MERCY JUSTICE, is bordered by the circular

182

(**187** Continued)

187

celebrated treaty of Penn with the Indians at Kensington the north suburb of Philadelphia, in 1682, and protected from firewood hunters by the British General Simcoe's sentry in the Revolution, blew down in 1810 at an age of 283 years.

Quail. 177. (*Colinus virginianus.*)

Prolific, ground-nesting, nonmigratory, gathering in winter coveys, preserved by game laws, rising for the sportsman with explosive whirring of wings, the quail cheers summer with his lively "bob white" note. How did the now meadow-loving bird subsist in the earlier days of the great meadowless forests?

177

John Fitch's Steamboat. 189.

The mosaic shows John Fitch experimenting in 1785 with his model steamboat on a pond near Hartsville in Bucks county. Boats having been propelled by crank paddle wheels turned by men or oxen since Roman times, and

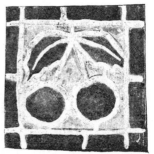

189

several attempts having been made to move boats with imperfect steam engines (Blasco de Gary, Barcelona 1543, Dennis Papin, Cassel 1707, De Juffroy, Lyons 1783), the finished practical steamboat resulted from several attempts at the end of the 18th century to apply the newly invented steam engine of Watt to the propulsion of water vehicles. Rumsey, Virginia 1786, tried propulsion by water jets. After several experiments in steam propulsion by oar and paddle wheels between 1785 and '90, and a screw propeller in 1796, John Fitch's idea was condemned by Franklin and a committee. Symington having practically applied Watt's engine to a towing steamer on the Clyde Canal in 1802, was condemned and discouraged by the canal company. Robert Fulton after being condemned by Napoleon's committee in 1803 at Paris, when proposing an invasion of England by steamboat, succeeded practically in applying Watt's engine to his paddle boat, the Clermont, (1807) on the Hudson, seventeen years after Fitch's oared steamboat (1790) had carried passengers from Philadelphia to Bristol, and nine years after the despairing suicide of Fitch at Bardstown Kentucky in 1798.

Cherries. 193. (*Prunus cerasus.*)

Rival of the strawberry, beloved of boys and birds, associated with the flavor of cherry bounce and pie, the delicious European fruit in its best known forms of pie, oxheart, or black cherry, when freshly imported and grown by the log cabin of the

193

pioneer, may have been seen by the Indian before his expulsion from Pennsylvania. The Pennsylvanian must thank the horticulture of his European ancestors for this fair fruit of early summer, brought to Europe by Lucullus the Roman epicure, from Cerasus of Asiatic

Pontus, to be cultivated for centuries in France England and Germany; and which if in Pennsylvania degenerating in flavor, has not failed in the magnificence of its white blossoms. These gladden the road sides when the meadow lark sings his spring song, and only yield in beauty to those which the Japanese wonder at on April seventh.

Chimney Swallow. 192. (*Chætura pelagica.*) Continually on the wing, flying at the rate of a mile a minute, skimming the pond's brim, dipping under water, or darting close to the meadow grass for insect prey,

192

master in the matchless gift of flight, the short-tailed long-winged dusky chimney swallow (properly a swift) must have ceased gluing his nest of twigs to the walls of caves and hollow trees, and resorted to the previously unknown farm house chimneys about 1720.

Penn's Seal of Bucks County. 211. A shield with three balls the arms of Penn, overshadowed by a tree, and inclosed by a leafy grapevine, is surrounded with the legend WILLIAM PENN PROPRIETOR AND GOVERNOR BUCKS.

211

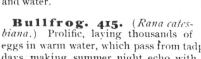

Lost and forgotten until rediscovered stamped in wax upon an old deed in the Court House at Doylestown.

Robin. 331. (*Merula migratoria.*) A few boys in the year 1908 begin to feel that when on the fairest morn of May, the redbreast sings among the apple blossoms, the sight and sound are worth all the cherries the bird may afterwards eat. But an older human generation had to be influenced to cease robin killing by opening the insect-filled stomach of the songster to reassure that of the man. Robins eat insects, and insects eat fruit, therefore robins help man to eat more fruit.

331

The Kingfisher. 420. (*Ceryle alcyon.*) The man with country boyhood, who learned to swim where the still water runs deep in the "horse hole," or by the roaring breast of the old mill dam, can never forget the echoing trumpet of the kingfisher, as the restless big headed black collared bird, flashing, diving, perching, sets going the wild echoes of woods air and water.

420

Bullfrog. 415. (*Rana catesbiana.*) Prolific, laying thousands of eggs in warm water, which pass from tadpole to frog in early summer days, making summer night echo with his deep bellowing, feeding

415

(**415** Continued)

upon insects snails and reptiles, the bullfrog has rather increased than diminished in numbers since the destruction of the great forest.

Indian Carving. 419. One of the series of carvings referring to animals birds and reptiles, possibly a panther, pecked with sharp stones by Indians upon the side of a boulder, known as Little Indian Rock, at Safe Harbor

on the Susquehanna.

Indian Rock Carvings. 410. The mosaic shows a few of the scattered figures of men animals and bird tracks, which, together with forms of reptiles and demonic symbols, were made probably

419

by Susquehannock, Delaware or Iroquois Indians, by pecking with hard sharp stones on the face of three large water-worn boulders in mid-Susquehanna at Safe Harbor. The grinding of driftwood in freshets slowly erases these weird symbols of a vanished race placed in the midst of roaring and dangerous rapids.

410

Song Sparrow. 418. (*Melospiza fasciata.*) Below the ripples where the mill stream lingers by bridge or eddy, and where the jet black water beetles dart upon

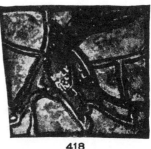

418

the odoriferous pool, the song sparrow, seizing a branch of hazel, or topmost fresh-leaved spray of willow, outvieing all his kindred, stirs the heart with his sweetest keynote of spring.

Eel. 414. (*Anguilla vulgaris.*) Living in water, burrowing in submarine mud, or traversing grass fields, covered with a green scaleless skin, the slippery eel, defying the boy's hand

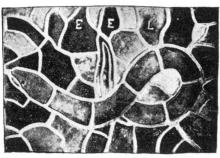

414

clutch, bites at the flannel wrapped string of the fisherman "bobbing for eels," seizes the baited strings floated over night on shingles in the mill-dam, or, twisted upon the boy's fishing line, rises from the "horse hole" instead of the expected catfish.

The Grasshopper. 417. Sweet as the song of the meadow lark, or scent of new mown hay, charming the recollection of

thousands of human minds aged in the toil of cities, rises the universal memory of an infant form, hatless and barefoot, chasing the ever present grasshopper, who with immense fascinating leaps wins the race on the soft grass or prickly stubble fields of summer. The "grasshopper war," an exterminating battle of an old Delaware and Susquehanna Valley myth, came, according to the farmer's wife's tale, from the overleaping by a grasshopper of

417

a sinew boundary stretched between two Indian camps. The chasing children of the rival tribes quarrel, and the squaws take their part, followed by the braves, till a desperate resulting battle strews the river shores, as at Durham, or fills the mound, as at Connewago, with skulls.

Indian Turtle. 413. One of nearly two hundred carvings of birds, animals, their tracks and reptiles, pecked with sharp stones by Indians in precolumbian times, against the side of Little Indian Rock, in the Susquehanna rapids at Safe Harbor. The turtle is represented with extended legs, as used for the Totemic badge of one of the three clans of the Lenni Lenape, or Delaware Indians.

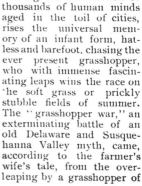

413

Weasel. 408. (*Putorius noveboracensis.*) Sometimes turning all white in winter, brown-backed, keen-scented, night-hunting, wholesale destroyer and blood-sucker of rats mice frogs birds and chickens.

408

Rabbit. 403. (*Lepus floridanus.*) With brown cinnamon and grey fur, and white under

tail, very prolific, subsisting on roots and vegetables, burrowing, crouching till almost touched, very fleet, doubling to escape dogs, the rabbit defies extermination in spite of gunners in season, minks weasels crows and hawks. Hard is the heart, which, unmoved to pity, sees the trembling rabbit crouching by a log or weed stalk, while the dogs bark and race in distant circles.

Rattlesnake. 404. (*Crotalus horridus.*) Less poisonous than the cobra of India, or the fer de lance of Martinique,

403

404

(**404** Continued)

devourer of small rodents, the deadly rattlesnake, where he survives in the Appalachians from New Hampshire to Florida, is justly dreaded by man. About four feet long, sluggish, coiling, rattling, reluctantly striking, the brown or blackish yellow diaper-striped snake, was avoided and venerated by Indians and white men, and but very rarely conciliated by snake loving mountaineers, who dare to pick up the fanged reptile in their hands.

Indian Rock Carving.

409. One of nearly 200 other figures, probably an elk, pecked with sharp stones by Indians, against the sides of three boulders known as Little Indian Rock, Big Indian Rock, and a third unnamed stone, in the Susquehanna rapids at Safe Harbor.

409

Mole. 405. (*Scalops aquaticus.*) Devourer not of roots or plants, but of earth worms, with gimlet nose, almost invisible min-

405

ute eyes, glossy silver grey fur, and powerful hairless clawed hands, the mole wedges and delves a little tunnel close under the summer sod, or deeper under frost, where his heaps of excavated earth rise to the surface to mark his work. Not where the truckman grumbles at young vegetable roots dried by the uplift of these undermining tunnels, nor where the man with the lawn mower and rake artificializes nature in village or suburb, but where by the old "barn bridge" generations of geese and sheep have pastured upon the venerable sod, may the observer mark with pleasure, ramifying lines of darker green shadows, penciled upon the turf, tracing the upswelling vaults of the moles' galleries that settle back after a rain.

406

Soft Shelled Crab. 406. (*Callinectes hastatus.*)

The maritime blue crab in its shell (hard shell), or having recently cast its shell in summer (soft shell), inhabits the muddy beaches of the Delaware Chesapeake and Atlantic tide water coasts. Deviled, broiled, fried, hashed, dressed in many ways, it ranks, like the terrapin oyster and canvasback duck as a boasted national dish.

Indian Rock Carving. 411.

One of the animal figures pecked by

411

Indians by pounding with sharp stones, against the smooth freshet-worn eastern side of a large boulder, known as Big Indian Rock, in the middle of the rapids of the Susquehanna at Safe Harbor.

Box Tortoise. 407. (*Cistudo carolina.*) Celebrated in white man's story and legend, venerated as an emblem of wisdom by the

Indian, the sluggish unwieldy reptile, heavily armored above and below by carapace and plastron, resists without much effort, the attack of many enemies; sometimes defying the tearing of the eagle's beak and talons, as when, if the legend be true, a bird of prey high in air, killed the Greek poet Aeschylus by dropping a tortoise upon his head.

407

The Raccoon. 412. (*Procyon lotor.*) Cousin to the bear, hibernating in winter, feeding on shellfish mussels birds turtle eggs insects nuts fruits frogs and corn, soaking its food in water, this gray-brown animal with white-striped tail, dwelling in trees, hunting at night, and a good swimmer, is easily tamable as a pet by man, who has not exterminated him in Pennsylvania.

Indian Panther. 416. One of the animal figures, probably a panther, pecked by Indians by pounding with sharp stones against the smooth, freshet-worn, eastern side of a large boulder, known as Big Indian

412

Rock, in the middle of the rapids of the Susquehanna at Safe Harbor.

Potter Terrapin. 330. (*Pseudemys rugosa.*) Having learned to eat tortoises in general from the Indian, who continually roasted them

416

on open fires, the white man digs the hibernating red-bellied terrapin from the winter mud of fresh water streams, and, throwing him alive into boiling water, cleans cooks and eats him, eggs and all. Outranking for man's food, all national dishes, save the canvasback duck, the reptile is threatened with extermination in Pennsylvania, where he is easily confused with the yet more esteemed salt water terrapin (*Malacoclemmys palustris*).

330

When the meat of the latter sells at from five to seven dollars per quart in Philadelphia, the vendor may stir in fifty to seventy per cent. of the bones flesh and eggs of the "potter," whereupon few epicures can detect the cheat.

Apples. 93. (*Malus.*)

Originally produced in Persia, the apple of the north temperate zone, now Americanized, may well contest its claim to be the greatest of the world's fruits, with the orange of the tropics.

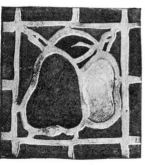

93

The Butterfly. 184.

Through one of the most marvelous changes in nature, sometimes lasting over winter, by way of egg laid upon a twig, voracious leaf-eating, skin-molting caterpillar, pseudo-death as a grub-mummy wrapped in self-made coffin, long sleep and gorgeous resurrection, the sun-loving, honey-seeking butterfly, cancelling in winged beauty the caterpillar's harm, emerges upon the lap of summer, to outvie the fairest of her flowers.

184

Franklin and the Kite. 180.

Experimenting with electricity during a thunder storm, in the fields near Philadelphia in June 1752, Franklin drew an electric spark down a kite string attached to a key. A world-celebrated experiment, suggesting lightning rods, and foreshadowing the telegraph.

180

The Pine. 194.

Represented by about 39 related species in the United States, shallow rooted, evergreen, highly valued for its wood, distilled for turpentine and pitch, darkening the Rocky mountain slopes or sandy seacoast, whispering in varied æolian tones, and as the white pine (*Pinus strobus*), rivaling in beauty the cedar of Lebanon or the Deodar of India, the tree in the form of the white pine rapidly destroyed by axe and saw, awaits its last chance of preservation, as a tree kept for ornament.

194

Pears. 198. (*Pyrus communis.*)

Rival of the apple, and perhaps surpassing the peach and apricot, unknown in prehistoric America, cultivated from the large wild native tree of Europe and Asia, dwarfed by grafting on the quince, the transatlantic pear has been a garden favorite since the days of Pliny and Virgil. Highly perfected in France and the Netherlands, under glass or upon trellises, it has been generally neglected in Pennsylvania, where it yet excels as the sweet yellow Bartlett, or the remarkable aromatic and unique Seckel. The latter, probably the most original fruit ever produced in the United States, originated in a pear tree, grown by

198

chance before 1800 close within the confluence of the Delaware and Schuylkill Rivers. Brought to the world's attention by the land owner Lawrence Seckel about 1800. Blew down in 1904.

Bumble Bee. 159. (*Bombus vagans.*) Indigenous to America. Making honey-lined nests in small colonies underground, and

when attacked by boys slashing shingle paddles bored with holes or leafy branches, defending its home to the death. Fertilizing flowers, carrying honey and wax as it hums in the sunbeams, buzzing for liberty against glass windows, or boring tunnels in the wood of old window sills, the American bee, undomesticated and unhived, like his honey-producing cousin imported from Europe, remains wild to vie with the butterfly, locust and dragon-fly as one of the chief delights of summer's fairest days.

159

The Blue Jay. 195. (*Cyanocitta cristata.*) The trumpet cry of the blue jay startles the quiet woods, while his blue wings gleam through the leaf shadows, as upon his omnivorous search for food, he seizes the autumnal chestnut, or in spring, devours young birds and steals bird eggs no less remorselessly than the ornithologist multiplies his skins for the cabinet, or the lady distorts his stuffed form, glass-eyed, upon her hat.

195

Beaver. 24. (*Castor canadensis.*) While the prolific subterranean muskrat, delivered

from his terrible enemy the mink, multiplies in the midst of civilization, the sensitive beaver instantly shrinks from contact with the human invader, who has almost exterminated him in Pennsylvania. The story of his matchless skill becomes a half-forgotten school boy's fable, and common knowledge no longer testifies to the fact that the animal resembling an enormous heavy tailed muskrat, gnaws down trees so as to lock them across streams, thereby forming driftwood dams with sufficient water for his island village.

24

Felling the Forest. 191. Neither steam car trolley automobile coal or iron mine oil or gas well probably worked the terrestrial change, suddenly produced, when the white colonist, with resounding blows of the long bitted axes of his ancestors, first dissipated the immemorial tree shade of the great forest. As the ancient red American retired or perished, houses cities and villages rose. Then the chimney swallow nested in its first chimney, the purple martin in its first man-made toyhouse, and the wren in a man prepared calabash. The quail and lark left the forest for open fields of man-planted grass. The crow first robbed the farmer's corn, the prolific muskrat, liberated by farmer's trap from his mink enemy, overpopulated the banks of mill

191

ponds, the housefly first buzzed in the log horse stable, and the European house rat overran the region, while the watercress of the old world invaded springs newly sunlit, and a hundred new European flowers sprang up by freshly cleared roads.

Wild Turkey. 181. (*Meleagris gallopavo.*) The wild turkey approaches extermination in the Eastern United States, by modern

North Americans who have sought to domesticate no wild native creature. In the closely related form of its Mexican cousin, origin of our farmyard Christmas bird, it was domesticated by prehistoric New Mexican cliff dwellers and Aztecs, and went to Europe with the Spaniards. Bred in the farmyards of Italy, England, Germany and France, and illustrated in the paintings of Bassano in the 16th century, the turkey, called "welsch hahn" and "indianer" in Germany, "dandon" in France, and miscalled after the Sultan's country in the land of its birth, came back to the new world by way of the old.

181

Oak Leaves. 196. (*Quercus.*) Long lived, colossal, durable, with color-producing bark, and sawdust highly valued by the carpenter. The slow growing oak, though unknown in Australia and tropical Africa, with various Ameri-

196

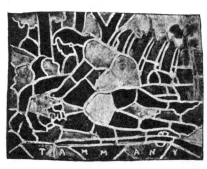

can forms as the black, red, pin, white and swamp oak, ennobles the forests of Asia, Europe and America in the north temperate zone. The familiar ashen-barked white oak was the frequently named land mark in old deeds.

The Death of Tammany. 185. A very old Indian said to be the celebrated Tammanend, head chief so-named of the Lenni Lenape (Dela-

185

ware) Indians, (deposed in 1718 and succeeded by Chief Allumpees) according to local tradition, committed suicide on the banks of Neshaminy Creek about 1750, and was buried there upon territory which he himself had sold to Penn in 1683. A political society in New York adopted his name.

Pears. 192. (*Pyrus communis.*) Rival of the apple, and perhaps surpassing the peach and apricot, unknown in prehistoric America, cultivated from the large

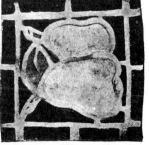

192

wild native tree of Europe and Asia, dwarfed by grafting on the quince, the transatlantic pear has been a garden favorite since the days of Pliny and Virgil. Highly perfected in France and the Netherlands, under glass or upon trellises, it has been generally neglected in Pennsylvania, where it yet excels as the sweet yellow Bartlett, or the remarkable aromatic and unique Seckel. The latter probably the most original fruit ever produced in the United States, originated in a pear tree grown by chance before 1800, close within the confluence of the Delaware and Schuylkill Rivers. Brought to the world's attention by the land owner Lawrence Seckel, about 1800. Bore fruit in 1885. It blew down in 1904.

Clover Stripper. 188.

The farmer by means of shafts, pulls a wooden comb projecting from a wheeled box, across the clover field, thus tearing off the ripe seed-filled tops, which, as they clog the teeth, a boy rakes into the box. Predecessor and type of all

188

reaping machines, lacking only the transverse knives. Described as for reaping wheat or rye when drawn by oxen, by Pliny. Surviving in Germany and probably France through the middle ages. Brought to America and used among Pennsylvania Germans until 1840.

Seal of Philadelphia 1701. 200. A shield quartered with figures

200

of clasped human hands scales a wheat sheaf and a ship, is bordered by the circular inscription SEAL OF THE CITY OF PHILADELPHIA 1701.

Rivetting Steel Plate. 214. Two plates of wrought steel, perforated with superposed holes, are rolled in the grip of a powerful machine, which, dropping hot rivets into the adjusted orifices, squeezes flat (clinches) the ends above and below by heavy pressure.

214

Wolf. 205. (*Canis occidentalis.*) Hunting in winter packs, running down foxes and smaller animals, or destroying the larger disabled elk or moose, howling, burrowing, always hungry, tamed by savages, and part ancestor of the friendly dog, the American gray wolf, devourer of sick bison, bison calves and domestic cattle, has been

205

222

Grapes. 222. The European grape, having produced wine for eighteen centuries, was transplanted to the garden of the Pennsylvanian farmer and generally neglected. Though remaining sweet and edible, so as to outrival the native fox and chicken grape, or flavor a home-brewed sugared acid wine, whether deteriorated by soil climate or lack of skill, in spite of extensive efforts in California New Jersey New York etc., the grape no longer (1908), produces for the American the ancient drink of his European ancestors.

more easily driven off and exterminated than his fierce cousin of northern Europe.

School Out. 210. With the inspiring hubbub that Eugene Aram heard, and less loud in country than in city, the pent up boys and girls, let loose from school recess, play leap frog, tag, prisoner's base, marbles, tipcat, catch ball, and jump rope, dig the gutter sand, mark play houses with rows of stones and flags of chicken

210

feathers, or garnish the trunks of trees with wild flowers.

The Pine. 226. Sawed for boards, hard or soft, white or yellow, origin of pitch, scored for exuding resin, the pine tree covers the northern hills and southern swamps. In the distinctive form of the beautiful white pine (*Pinus strobus*), rivalling the cedar of Lebanon or the Deodar of India, with its bare winglike limbs feathered only at the ends, the valuable tree, cut with the axe or movable saw, and floated down stream in the form of trimmed logs, seems to approach extermination.

226

Fall of the Primeval Forest. 207. The Latin inscription ARBORES CADUNT EMERGNT HOMINES, with its third word abbreviated, (translated, trees fall men rise), refers to the immense change worked upon man and nature, when one of the greatest forests of the globe first yielded its shadow to the sunlight.

207

The House of Steel. 204. A fantastic serrated profile, as of castles and palaces, rises dream-like in the distance, where walls of immense height tower above windy highways, narrow in proportion, as the mediæval streets of old Europe. The vision fades as you approach, and enter scaffolds of Pennsylvanian steel, veneered with

(**204** Continued)

,crusts of stone or brick, partitioned monotonously in fifteen or twenty congested layers (stories), of duplicated steam-heated pigeon holes (offices), where the modern American city, having overcrowded the earth, rises to the sky.

204

Husking Corn. 201. No machine having yet been invented to husk maize, the farmer, having thrown the unbound shock of stalks, cleared from

the "horse" stiffened stack upon the ground, still (1908) kneels in the cold autumnal days as his colonial ancestor did, upon the dry stalks, tearing the husk from the ear by means of a peg of iron or wood strapped to the mid fingers of the right hand, and projecting between thumb and forefinger.

201

Shoemaker. 203. Before the days of country stores or shoe factories, the itinerant farm-hand shoemaker lodging at the farm house, bringing leather from the country tannery, carrying his tools with him, and finding lasts in the garret, made shoes for the family.

The Crow. 202. (*Corvus americanus.*) Not from his striking color and figure, his anatomy or his habits according to the bird book, might the nonmigrating, incomparably sagacious, grain-eating crow claim distinction, but rather from the fact that he stands supreme among birds, as victorious in an eternal life struggle against the human maxim, man-condemned but man-practiced, that might makes right. Marshalled in de-

203

structive flocks, guided, guarded and generalled, scouting, watching, venturing, despising the scarecrow, evading trap and poison, guaging gun range as it extends, the ever-present crow, defying the northern winter, despoils the human spoiler, from the exact standpoint of the latter.

Pears. 227. (*Pyrus communis.*) Rival of the apple, and perhaps surpassing the peach and apricot, unknown in prehistoric America, cultivated from the large wild

202

227

(**227** Continued)

native tree of Europe and Asia, dwarfed by grafting on the quince, the transatlantic pear has been a garden favorite since the days of Pliny and Virgil. Highly perfected in France and the Netherlands, under glass or upon trellises, it has been generally neglected in Pennsylvania, where it yet excels as the sweet yellow Bartlett, or the remarkable aromatic and unique Seckel. The latter, probably the most original fruit ever produced in the United States, originated in a pear tree grown by chance before 1800, close within the confluence of the Delaware and Schuylkill Rivers. Brought to the world's attention by the land owner Lawrence Seckel, about 1800. It blew down in 1904.

The Sunfish. 317. Where the meadow brook deepens under hazel bushes, or plunges into the the milldam's pool, or where sunbeams piercing the warped boards of the old byroad bridge, illumine the scented water, barefooted children, with worm boxes poles strings pin hooks and puppy, peeping downward, behold the sunfish, akin to humanity in its eyes, fanning itself with winglike fins, a translucent

317

golden shadow in an enchanted water world.

Thrashing With the Flail. 190. With a heavy club, loosely tied (sometimes fastened with a hickory swivel) to the end of a staff, the farmers, by an ancient method surviving from Roman times, club the grain from the wheat stalks. The familiar measured drumming sound of flails on the barn floor, generally superseded by the whirr of thrashing machines worked by horse treadmills, about 1860. The flail still (1908) used occasionally for rye, the

190

desirable straws of which are too much torn by the thrashing machine.

Plover. 218. (*Aegialitis vocifera.*) Everywhere familiar with its cry of "killdeer," its sensational flutterings, and feignings of lameness along meadow or pond, the long-legged, red eye-lidded, white collared plover, unmindful of cow or horse, demonstrates its love for eggs nest or young, by misleading in vain chase the destructive boy or bounding puppy in the hatching days of spring.

218

Skating. 302. The paintings of Ostade and Teniers show the sport of skating flourishing in Holland before the settlement of Pennsylvania. Introduced as a boyish sport by first settlers with metal

(302 Continued)

skates and derived from earlier boys' practice of propelling themselves across ice
by thrusts of spiked staves, upon animals'
shin bones strapped to the feet. Before
1856 very long steel projections of the skate
runner curled back over the skater's toe.

302

Apples. 220. (*Malus.*) Originally
produced in Persia, the apple of the north
temperate zone, now Americanized, may
well contest its
claim with the
orange of the
tropics to be the
greatest of the
world's fruits.

220

Red-Bird. 219. (*Cardinalis cardinalis.*) Vivid, scarlet-crested, heavy-
billed, active, non-migratory, named from
the scarlet robe of the Catholic high
ecclesiastic, most conspicuous of songsters,
lurking in summer in
chosen wet bramble
thickets, or flashing
hope and warmth into the drab woods of winter,
the cardinal bird, rich in song, is often seen imprisoned for life in a small cage.

219

School In. 209. Before 1830, many
school masters from Scotland taught Pennsylvania's English speaking youth, in school houses
of logs, or octagonal buildings with desks ranged
round the walls, and warmed by cast iron
("Dutch" warming, or later "ten-plate" warming and heating)
stoves placed in the middle. The organizing of public schools with
compulsory English instruc-
tion in 1840, superseding the
older German schools in the
Pennsylvania German dis-
tricts, ended the art of Fractur, or illuminated writing,
and the punishment of the
bocks brille (goats' spectacles), worn by bad boys
when thrown at them by
the teacher.

209

Shad. 206. (*Clupea
sapidissima.*) Ascending
eastern seaboard rivers in
the spring to spawn, lost in
winter in the ocean's depth,
the sensitive graceful shad,
dying in captivity, or at the
friction of nets, immensely
prolific, migrating in shoals, protected by law, netted in the spring,
was fried in the long-handled frying
pan, broiled on the gridiron by the
open fire of the old farm kitchen, or
roasted on a plank by the bonfire of
the Delaware River fisherman.

The Sower. 212. An open-
mouthed bag hangs round the
sower's left shoulder, and his right

206

212

(212 Continued)

hand seizes and scatters the grain, in time measured with his steps, as he strides across the plowed harrowed and rolled field.

Penn's Seal of Pennsylvania. 225.
A shield with the arms of William Penn, against a background adorned with scrolls, and inscribed with the words "MERCY

225

JUSTICE," is bordered by the circular inscription WILLIAM PENN PROPRIETOR AND GOVERNOR OF PENNSYLVANIA.

310

The Elm. 310. (*Ulmus americana.*)
Less conspicuous and beloved for village shade than in New England, the white, American or water elm of Pennsylvania, often vase-shaped in the outline of its plumed branches, loves water courses and escapes the barbarism of Pennsylvania German village tree-topping, in moist woods. The most celebrated tree of its kind in Pennsylvania, venerated as shading the treaty of Penn with the Indians at Kensington in 1682, and protected from firewood hunters by the British General Simcoe's sentry in the Revolution, blew down in 1810 at an age of 283 years.

Mason and Dixon's Line. 300.
A series of marble posts inscribed each with a pair of small armorial shields, for William Penn and Lord Baltimore, (see specimens at Pennsylvania and Maryland Historical Societies), set five miles apart, and interplaced with less elaborate pillars, of which some still (1908) stand in place, marked the most celebrated boundary in the United States, surveyed by Charles Mason and Jeremiah Dixon between 1763 and 1767. The mosaic shows a negro workman setting one of the posts for the surveyors. Ever after regarded as dividing the territory customs and ideals of the north and south Atlantic States, dwelt upon during the Civil war in

300

speech and story, baptizing the whole southern region with the name "Dixie," the celebrated boundary is often recalled by the words and music of two superlatively American songs, "I'se Gwine to Dixie" by C. A. White, and the still better known "Way Down South in Dixie" by Daniel Emmett, ancestor of negro minstrels.

Reaping Machine. 301.
A large steel comb combs the grain stalks, at the same time cutting them by the cross horizontal

301

Factories. 216. Not architecture of beauty for man or state, but a stern confusion of irregular roofs, windy galleries, soot-dimmed windows and smoky towers, black gigantic and significant, rises against the sky above the modern city, to mark the dominance of machinery over human hand labor since 1820. Who shall measure the meaning of the nightly flash and perpetual roar, upon which the strength wealth comfort hope ignorance errors cruelty pride and success of modern humanity slowly advances to nobler things.

(**301** Continued)
slash of internal triangular double-edged knives. Developed from various inventions in England and America by the middle of the 19th century, based upon the grain comb minus knives described by Pliny, and surviving in Pennsylvania as the "clover stripper" (see No. 188), the reaping machine superseded the primeval sickle, and the mediæval cradle scythe, about 1830.

216

Reading the Declaration of Independence. 303. While the soldier, as seen in the mosaic, reads the Declaration of Independence, a statesman stands by him, typifying the rival claims of war and states craft to the founding of the nation, and the soldier's denial, that in the revolution of 1776, the pen was mightier than the sword.

Potter at the Wheel. 314. Pushing with his bare foot a large wooden horizontal fly wheel, or stick strapped to a crank under the table, the seated potter, supplied with wooden scoop, wet leather, soaked cloth, water box, etc., causes a ball of plastic clay to revolve on a wooden disk in the table top, and to rise

303

into bowl shape, at the pressure of his wet slippery fingers.

Blowing the Conch Horn. 313. Farther than the jingle of mule bells on the tow path, and above the roar of the locked sluice, comes at evening the muffled far reaching mellow sound of the conch horn, a punctured shell of *strombus gigans*, blown by the lip vibration of the canal boatman, as the mule-towed boat approaches the lock.

314

307

(**313** Continued)
Thus warned the dozing keeper opens the lock without loss of time, as the night end of the boatman's journey approaches. Still used (1908) on the Delaware and Lehigh canal.

The Telephone. 307.
The electric signalling of messages on wires, from great distances, was immensely enlarged in scope when man learned how to talk directly along wires at from one to three hundred miles distance. Telephone invented as a high development of the work of earlier inventors by Alexander Graham Bell 1874-1877.

313

Hoeing Corn. 309.
Maize, which will not ripen in the cool summers of England and North Germany, grows freely in the hot August suns of Pennsylvania. You helped the process by hoeing out the soil exhausting weeds, where between the corn stalks, because of interplanted beans or pumpkins, you dared not let a horse drag a cultivator. Hasten the work while the thunder cloud rolls overhead promising the refreshing help of summer rain. It was on the old field hoe with ferrule welded to blade, that a daub of plastered corn meal was baked into the negro's hoe cake over a bon fire.

Boys Playing Marbles. 316.
With little balls of burnt clay or glass, called marbles, and nicknamed "commies," "bullies," or "aggies," the boys shoot between thumb and forefinger (knuckles down) "bullies" and other marbles, in and out of circles or ellipses, inscribed on the smooth trodden earth of town commons foot paths or school grounds, Thus trolling for first shot into the ring (common marbles), or shooting from the circumference (bully in the ring), or in or out of heel holes at a hand span's distance, contending in earnest "for keeps" as little gamblers, or "in fun," whether winning or "strapped," they play an ancient game probably derived from bowls, familiar in eastern Europe in the 13th century. Brought to America from Britain. Played in Oldenburg Germany, and in Silesia (kugeln) about 1880.

309

316

Buttonwood. 308.
(*Platanus occidentalis.*) The huge sycamore tree, seventy to one hundred feet high, with conspicuous scaly bark, is decorated over winter with brown button-shaped fruit. Massive-limbed with open shade, early

308

346

bared in autumn, and with glittering bark spotted with green and gray, the tree was the farmer's choice of old to shade the spring house.

The Muskrat. 346. (*Fiber zibethicus.*) The amphibious prolific muskrat, inhabiting lakes and streams, invading cultivated lands, threatening dams and canals, destroying the water lily and lotus where they had flourished before, defies man's efforts to dig him out and exterminate him, and increases rather than disappears before the same civilization which, in exterminating the blood-letting mink, has withdrawn from his life struggle the muskrat's worst enemy.

304

Trotting Horse. 304. As the chief attraction of state and county fairs, and the prime occasion of bets prizes and purses, carefully bred horses, driven by jockey drivers in light wagons or carts (sulkies), race on tracks at about 140 seconds per mile. The sport characteristically American, in high favor about 1840-'80, now (1908) wanes in favor of horse races *run*, by horses with mounted jockeys.

311

Sweet Gum. 311. (*Liquidambar styraciflua.* The lofty erect sweet gum, with its burrlike brown winter fruit, winglets of corky bark skewered through its branches like the scales of an alligator, called liquid-ambar and alligator wood, is not so resinous as its Asiatic cousins, producing the storax gum. With its five-pointed leaves of unsurpassable beauty, it outvies the foliage of maple trees, in the flaming glory of its autumn color.

The Sheep. 356. No American animals or birds (save the dog and turkey trained by Indian or Eskimo), having been domesticated by white North Americans, and all other domesticated animals and birds now established in North America, having been tamed in the old world, not by civilized man, but by savages in the stone age, the sheep, contributor of wool clothing and mutton, and second only to the horse and cow as man's helper, Americanized by earliest settlers, came from Europe like the rest.

356

355

Grain Elevator. 355. Overarching the freight car on its track, and the ship in its dock, a lofty building receives the world's food, as grain, lifted into its storage bins, on running straps armed with boxes, to drop it again through tubes into ship or car, for further transfer or export. The Latin inscription NATIONIS GRANARIA is translated, granary of the nation.

Coal Breaker. 358. Grim uncouth fantastic, black with smoke and dust, a wooden structure with lofty windowed galleries rises against the sky. Through it the anthracite coal, lifted in masses from the mines of the Lehigh and Susquehanna, is crushed and run through various sieves, for "egg," "stove," "chestnut," "pea," "rice," and "buckwheat" sizes, to fall from aloft into cars.

Automobile. 353. When about 1900, the invention of light gasoline motor engines enabled the operation of road wagons by

358

mechanism at 20 miles or more per average hour, the now (1908) famous automobile appeared to revolutionize road traffic, improve highways, ease the toil of the horse, encroach upon the passenger transport of railroads, increase the personal contact of scattered individuals, and renew the city man's acquaintance with the country.

353

Camera and Photographer. 305. Photography the process rendered practical by Daguerre (1839) of staining the lights and shadows of natural objects in picture form upon sensitized glass, improved by reprinting from the glass picture upon sensitized paper, and developed by amateur experiments about 1885–1900, soon superseded older hand methods of picture making and picture reproducing. Marking the downfall of wood and steel engraving, the process while destroying certain forms of art, offsets the loss in its contribution to human progress.

305

Penn's Seal of Philadelphia. 312. The mosaic shows a group of conventionalized houses surrounded with the inscription WILLIAM PENN PROPRIETOR AND GOVERNOR PHILADELPHIA. Devised for William Penn about 1682.

John Fitch's Steamboat. 306. The mosaic shows John Fitch's oared steam passenger boat plying on the Delaware River from Philadelphia to Bristol in 1790, seventeen years before Fulton's "Clermont" succeeded upon the Hudson River, and six years before Symington's "Charlotte Dundas" towed canal boats on the Clyde Canal, yet 247 years after Blasco de Gary, 83

312

306

(**306** Continued)
years after Dennis
Papin, and 7 years
after de Jouffroy.
Many schoolboys in
the United States have
been erroneously
taught that Robert Ful-
ton invented the steam
boat. See page 73.

**Franklin's
Press. 352.** Print-
ing invented by the
Chinese as a process
of pressing sheets of
paper, by rubbing with

a hand brush or cloth, against inked groups
of assembled block letters. Reinvented by
the Germans, Guttenburg and Faust, about
1450, and revolutionized by the Swiss-
American Mergenthaler in 1895. Modern-
izing and vastly transforming human
thought since the 16th century, it employed the labor of Benjamin Franklin in
his earlier days.

Dragon Fly. 362. Believed to be
the "Doctor" or feeder of the water snake,

362

by the barefooted
country boy, as the
latter searches the
creek for bullfrogs,
or lifts with skilled
hand the unresisting
half-hypnotized mullet ("sucker") from his
water hole under the bank. The dragon fly in
several closely related family forms as "snake
feeder" or "mosquito hawk," emerging from an
early submarine life to cast its shell and take
wing, vies with the butterfly as a charmer of
children and type of the fire and
energy of mid summer.

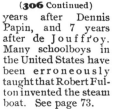

352

Rattlesnake. 366. (*Crotalus horridus.*) Less poisonous
than the cobra of India, or the
fer de lance of Martinique, devourer of small rodents, the
deadly rattlesnake, where he survives in the Appalachians from
from New Hampshire to Florida,
is justly
dreaded
by man.
About

366

four feet long, sluggish, coiling, rattling, reluctantly striking, the brown or blackish-
yellow diaper-striped snake, was avoided and
venerated by Indians and white men, and
but very rarely conciliated by snake-loving
mountaineers, who dare to pick up the
fanged reptile in their hands.

Flying Squirrel. 360. (*Sciuropterus volans.*) Nocturnal, dwelling in large
gnawed holes in dead trees, old house cornices, deserted garrets, or summer houses,

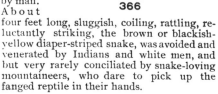

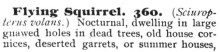

360

369

sometimes imprisoned in tin cages by the farmer's boy, the beautiful flying squirrel outvies in celebrity many larger animals, by flitting at night diagonally from tree to tree upon winglike extensions of its leg skin.

Gasometer. 369. A huge bolted sheet iron bottomless barrel-shaped vessel, floating by gas compression on a tank of water, and pressing illuminating gas through pipes into city and village houses. Since about 1830, illuminating gas, made from coal, has contended and still (1908) contends with electricity as a house and street light.

Plover. 361. (*Aegialitis vocifera.*) Everywhere familiar with its cry of "killdeer," its sensational flutterings and feignings of lameness along meadow or pond, the plover, unmindful of cow or horse, demonstrates its love of eggs nest and young, by misleading in vain chase, the destructive boy or bounding puppy in the hatching days of spring.

361

Potter Terrapin. 363. (*Pseudemys rugosa.* Having learned to eat tortoises in general from the Indian, who continually roasted them on open fires, the white man digs the hibernating red-bellied native terrapin from the submarine mud of fresh water streams, and throwing him alive into boiling water, cleans cooks and eats him eggs and all. Outranking for man's food all national dishes save the canvas-back duck, the reptile is threatened with extermination in Pennsylvania, where he is easily confused with the yet more esteemed salt water terrapin (*Malacoclemmys palustris*). When the meat of the latter sells for from five to seven dollars per quart in Phila-

363

delphia, the vendor may stir in fifty or seventy five per cent. of the bones flesh and eggs of the "potter," whereupon few epicures can detect the cheat.

Shad. 357. (*Clupea sapidissima.*) Netted while ascending in shoals eastern seaboard rivers in the spring to spawn, protected by law, lost in winter in the ocean's depth,

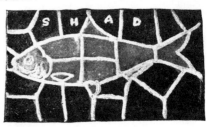

357

the immensely prolific sensitive graceful shad, dying in captivity or at the friction of nets, was fried in the long-handled frying pan, broiled on the gridiron by the open kitchen fire, or roasted on a plank, by the bonfire of the Delaware River fisherman.

Trolley Car. 351. Made practical after several previous inventions (Siemens and Halske,

351

Berlin 1879 and Van Depole and others about 1884), about 1885, running on tracks generally placed on city streets or country turnpikes, by a current of electricity passing through a wheeled iron rod sprung against an overhead wire. Boxed or open, windowed, heated, rapid, light and easily stopped, carrying freight and passengers from place to place, the electric railway car or trolley, has resulted in an immense outstretching of city and town life into the country, a great disturbance of rural conditions, and the ready introduction of the secluded farmer to town and city.

354

Mole. 354. (*Scalops aquaticus.*) Devourer, not of roots or plants, but of earth worms, with gimlet nose, almost invisible minute eyes, glossy silver gray fur, and powerful hairless clawed hands, the mole wedges and delves a little tunnel close under the summer sod, or deeper under frost, where his heaps of excavated earth rise to the surface to mark his work. Not where the truckman grumbles at young vegetable roots dried by the uplift of these undermining tunnels, nor where the man with the lawn mower and rake artificializes nature in village or graded suburb, but where by the old "barn bridge" geese and sheep pasture upon the ancient sod, may the observer mark with pleasure, the ramifying lines of darker green shadow, pencilled upon the turf, marking the upswelling vaults of the moles' galleries that settle back after a rain.

389

Gettysburg. 389. A struggle between citizens of the United States at Gettysburg in 1863, decided against the continued inconsistent existence of negro slavery in the liberty asserting United States, and against the division of the Republic into two nations.

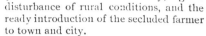

13

Reaping With the Sickle. 13. Lean forward and seizing a large bunch of wheat or rye with the left hand, cut the stalks near the ground, by drawing the keen serrated, narrow sickle blade across them from left to right. Then as the mosaic shows, you reap as your ancestors did from Egyptian times until about 1820, when at the advent of the European grain cradle or of the Hainault scythe (dispensing with stalk grasping), and finally the reaping machine, the greatest craft of husbandry changed suddenly and forever.

Washington Crossing the Delaware. 402. On Christmas night 1776, General Washington led the American army secretly in flatboats across the Delaware River, just above the present (1908) bridge at Morrisville, Bucks county, and surprising

402

the Hessian army employed by the British, defeated them at Trenton, and captured their General Rahl.

Rabbit. 371. (*Lepus floridanus.*) With brown cinnamon and gray fur, and white under tail, very prolific, subsisting on roots and vegetables, burrowing, crouching till almost touched, very fleet, doubling to escape dogs, the rabbit defies extermination, in spite of gunners in season, minks, weasels, crows and hawks. Hard is the heart which unmoved to pity, sees the terrified rabbit crouching by log or weed stalk, while the dogs bark and race in distant circles.

371

Potter Terrapin. 372. (*Pseudemys rugosa.*) Having learned

372

to eat tortoises in general from the Indian, who continually roasted them on open fires, the white man digs the hibernating red-bellied terrapin from the deep mud of fresh water streams, and throwing him alive into boiling water, cleans cooks and eats him, eggs and all. Outranking as man's food, all national dishes save the canvasback duck, the reptile is threatened with extermination in Pennsylvania, where he is easily confused with the yet more esteemed salt water terrapin (*Malacoclemmys palustris*). When the meat of the latter sells at from five to seven dollars per quart in Philadelphia, the vendor may stir in from fifty to seventy-five per cent. of the bones flesh and eggs of the "potter", whereupon few epicures can detect the cheat.

INDEX.

INDEX.

INDEX.

ERRATA

Page 46, Under No. 90
Page 94, Under No. 402
For Morrisville
Read Taylorsville